for Dick —
food + Shakespeare
Shakespeare + food

Lauren

Shakespeare's Kitchen

Shakespeare's Kitchen

RENAISSANCE RECIPES FOR
THE CONTEMPORARY
COOK

FRANCINE SEGAN

PHOTOGRAPHS BY TIM TURNER

RANDOM HOUSE | NEW YORK

LIBRARY OF CONGRESS CATALOGING-IN-PUBLICATION DATA
SEGAN, FRANCINE.
SHAKESPEARE'S KITCHEN: RENAISSANCE RECIPES
FOR THE CONTEMPORARY COOK/ FRANCINE SEGAN;
PHOTOGRAPHS BY TIM TURNER.—1ST ED.
P. CM.
ISBN 0-375-50917-8 (ALK. PAPER)
1. COOKERY, ITALIAN. I. TITLE.
TX723 .S377 2003
641.5945—DC21   2002036839

To my soul mate, Marc Segan,

our wonderful children, Samantha and Max,

and to my mother, Eleanor Oddo

Preface

SHAKESPEARE IS A FUNDAMENTAL PART OF OUR AMERICAN CULTURE, and we Americans have long had a fascination with his life and works. We quote him daily, often without knowing it. "By the book," "the be all and end all," "seen better days," "for goodness' sake," "not budge an inch," and "eaten me out of house and home" are all Shakespeare's words. His plays are produced more than those of any other writer in history. Hollywood has created hundreds of movies inspired by him, and countless theaters across America bring Shakespeare's plays to the stage each year.

America shares a culinary history with many nations, but foremost is England. The Pilgrims who arrived at Plymouth Rock were Shakespeare's contemporaries and they brought with them their cookbooks from England. In those early years there was no time for culinary innovation, so settlers adapted the recipes as best they could to the indigenous foods found in their new world.

At the time of our independence in 1776, America had not yet developed a unique culinary signature. In fact, it wasn't until 1796 that the first American cookbook, *American Cookery* by Amelia Simmons, was written and published on these shores. Until then all the cookbooks in America were European imports.

It is from the English that we inherit much of what we now think of as "American" food. Apple pie, stuffed turkey, and even gingerbread houses all originate in England. The roots of American cooking are to be found in Shakespeare's England.

It is impossible to turn back the clock and prepare dishes precisely as they were made in the sixteenth and seventeenth centuries. Spices, meat, fish, and vegetables have altered over the years with improved cultivation and scientific intervention. Cooking techniques have also changed considerably since Shakespeare's time. We no longer boil in cauldrons suspended from cranes over a hearth or bake in iron boxes and brick ovens. However, it is possible to achieve a fairly close approximation of the foods eaten four hundred years ago by taking Shakespeare's advice to "piece out our imperfections with [our] thoughts" (*King Henry V*).

The cookbooks published during the late 1500s and early 1600s provide a fascinating window into Shakespeare's world. They show not only how people cooked and ate, but also how they wrote and organized their thoughts. For example, Elizabethan recipes were written as running text and did not include the details we are used to seeing in modern cookbooks, such as recipe titles and ingredient lists. Similarly, Shakespeare's plays were also originally written and published without the numbered acts and scenes we are so accustomed to today.

In those days, cookbook authors assumed that the chef knew the proper proportions of ingredients, so quantities were rarely specified. "As your eye shall advise you" or "as your cook's mouth shall serve him" was as specific as they got. When quantities were mentioned it was with colorful and sometimes vague references such as "four penny worth of Saffron," "little cakes as broad as a shilling," and "cut as thick as a half crown piece."

There were no cooking thermometers for measurements more precise than "beware you burn it not" and "sufficiently bak't." Clocks and timepieces, expensive in Shakespeare's day, were rarely found in kitchens, so that cooking times either were not expressed or were given in other terms such as "you will know it is cooked when it sticks to the spoon" or, as an Italian cookbook of the period notes, "cook for no more than two Our Fathers."

In *Shakespeare's Kitchen,* the original text is included for many recipes, with spelling, grammar, syntax, and punctuation left intact. Spelling was not yet standardized in Shakespeare's day, so you may find the same word spelled differently even within the same recipe. Pie may be "pye," flour "flower," and raisins anything from "raysons" to "raisyns."

Some instructions sound amusing to our modern ears, for example, "Thrust your Knife into the flesh of your Legge down as deep, as your finger is long."

Charming phrases in these old recipes include:

"Brush off the golde with the foot of an hare or conie." Gold was commonly used in cooking and a rabbit's foot often served as a basting brush.

"Eggs in Moon Shine." Moonshine was a fanciful term for the white sauce in this dish and had nothing to do with liquor, home-brewed or otherwise.

"Put in a little piece of butter as much as a walnut," "as much white salt as will into an Egshell," and "make the balls as big as nutmeg or musket bullet," or as "big as a tennis ball" are all terms used by the Elizabethans to describe quantities by reference to familiar objects.

Although I have taken recipes from many different sixteenth- and seventeenth-century cookbooks, I do have a few favorite authors. I borrowed heavily from Robert May's *Accomplisht Cook,* in part because his is by far the largest cookbook of the era with thirteen hundred recipes, but also because he is clearly a cook's cook, a professional chef, unlike other authors, who were writers first and cookbook writers only second. Robert May was a professional full-time chef to the nobility who began his cooking apprenticeship at age twelve with his father, also a career chef.

Robert May wrote his first and only cookbook in 1660 at age seventy. His recipes span several decades of culinary history, back to Shakespeare's day and even to Medieval styles of dining and food preparation. Robert May speaks lovingly of the bygone era of elaborate preparations for noblemen's special feasts "before good House-keeping had left England."

Most chapters in *Shakespeare's Kitchen* showcase a particular Elizabethan cookbook writer. In the Basics chapter, you will meet cookbook author, poet, and inventor Sir Hugh Plat, who was knighted by King James I for his innovations in agriculture. In the Desserts chapter ("The Banquet") you'll get to know Sarah Longe, who shares recipes enjoyed by Queen Elizabeth I and King James I; and in the Appetizers chapter you will meet Gervase Markham, whose 1615 cookbook begins: "Eating and drinking are a very pretty invention."

Allow me to introduce you to these wonderful Elizabethan cooks, their recipes, and the foods and dining customs of sixteenth- and seventeenth-century Europe as we journey back to Shakespeare's England and back to our culinary roots.

Acknowledgments

MY DEEPEST GRATITUDE TO Mary Bahr, Judi Carle, and Tim Turner for their expert guidance and wonderful insights throughout every step of the process.

Appreciation to Agatha and Valentina Gourmet Food in New York City; Louis Balducci; Elise Abrams Antiques, Great Barrington, Massachusetts; Lock Stock and Barrel Gourmet Foods and Wine Merchants, Great Barrington, Massachusetts; Kuttner Prop Rental and The Prop Company in New York City. Thanks to Allison Fishman, Marcia Kiesel, Wes Martin, Judy Singer, Lee Elman, Bob and Toni Strassler, Laura Chester, Honey Sharp Garden Design, Berkshire Botanical Garden, Windy Hill Nursery, Adrian Van Zon, Dorothy Denburg, Moira Hodgson, Bill Rice, Elliot Brown, Nach Waxman, and Professor Roger Deakins.

Special thanks to the New York Public Library, Rare Books Division; Astor, Lenox and Tilden Foundations; the Huntington Library; the Folger Shakespeare Library; and to Arlene Shaner, New York Academy of Medicine Library, Malloch Rare Books Room.

And most important, thank you to Shakespeare festivals everywhere for keeping us connected to Shakespeare's works, as the Bard would have most wanted, with live actors on a real stage.

Contents

*I*N *SHAKESPEARE'S KITCHEN*, THE READER AND FOOD LOVER IS GIVEN a unique introduction to William Shakespeare and the culture of his era. Since Shakespeare so passionately glorified eating and drinking in his plays and verse, food provides an ideal medium for approaching his life.

As a student of theater in college I often had difficulty wading through Shakespeare's works. Unraveling the many layers of meaning in his writing was often a daunting and oblique task, rather like cracking the code of an ancient puzzle. If *Shakespeare's Kitchen* had been available then, it might have provided a delicious entrée into the era in which he lived.

The French philosopher and food writer Brillat-Savarin said, "Tell me what you eat and I will tell you what you are." *Shakespeare's Kitchen* not only reveals, sometimes surprisingly, what people were eating in Shakespeare's time but also provides recipes that today's cooks can easily re-create with readily available ingredients.

It has been said that one who knows food also knows history, language, and culture. This book on the food of Shakespeare's era beautifully illustrates that truth. Included are fascinating introductions to the recipes that offer a unique perspective on daily life in England during the sixteenth century, illustrative stories of Elizabethan entertaining that depict a charming spirit of fun and frivolity, and many historical references that shed light on the numerous influences of foreign countries and cultures.

There is something unmistakably quaint and distinctive about an old, authentic recipe. The taste of the food draws you back to a different time much like wearing a period costume or entering an ancient space does. These recipes cause one to reflect on what it might have felt like to be alive during this colorful and vibrant time.

Shakespeare's Kitchen offers up an edible historical narrative from which food lovers, history buffs, and Shakespearean scholars will all derive nourishment.

Shakespeare's Kitchen

Rickshaws: Appetizers

. . . .

Kickshaws, the Elizabethan misspelling of the French *quelque chose,* "a little something," refers to dishes we now categorize as appetizers or hors d'oeuvres.

The 1615 cookbook *The English Huswife*, by Gervase Markham, begins, "Now the compound Fricases, are those which consist of manie things such as Tansies, Fritters, Pancakes, and anie Quelquechose whatsoever, being things of great request and estimation in France, Spaine, and Italy, and the most curious Nations."

Taking recipes from *The English Huswife* and from other cookbooks, this chapter offers a sampling of kickshaws from throughout Renaissance Europe.

Beef Purses

SERVES 8

> I picked and cut most of their festival purses; and had not the old man
> come in with whoo-bub against his daughter and
> the king's son and scared my choughs from the chaff,
> I had not left a purse alive in the whole army.

THE WINTER'S TALE, 4.4

*I*N SHAKESPEARE'S DAY, meat turnovers like these were called "purses" because they looked like the small change holders people wore attached to their belts. The expression "cut purse" referred to a thief who cut the cord to steal the purse, an all too common occurrence in those days before policed streets.

The savory filling of tangy candied ginger and sweet dried fruit make these purses worth stealing! Enjoy them with a glass of cold ale before heading off to see your favorite production of Shakespeare or while watching one of the many great movies inspired by his work.

8 ounces ground round or ground sirloin

¼ teaspoon ground rosemary

⅓ cup currants

6 pitted dates, finely chopped

1 tablespoon finely chopped candied ginger

¼ teaspoon ground cinnamon

¼ teaspoon freshly ground nutmeg

2 tablespoons light brown sugar

½ teaspoon salt

Pinch of freshly milled black pepper

½ recipe of Renaissance Dough (page 239)

1 large egg, beaten

1. Place the beef, rosemary, currants, dates, ginger, cinnamon, nutmeg, brown sugar, salt, and pepper in a bowl and mix well. Refrigerate for at least 6 hours, or overnight. Remove the meat mixture from the refrigerator 1 hour before baking.

2. Preheat the oven to 350°F. Roll out the Renaissance Dough ⅛ inch thick on a floured work surface. Using a 3-inch round ring cutter, cut out 24 dough circles. Place 1½ tablespoons of the meat mixture on each circle, fold in half, and pinch the edges to seal. Brush the purses with the egg and place on a well-greased nonstick baking sheet. Bake for 15 minutes, or until golden brown.

ORIGINAL RECIPE:

To make pursses or Cremitaries

Take a little mary, small raysons, and Dates, let the stones bee taken away, these being beaten together in a Morter, season it with Ginger, Sinemon, and Sugar, then put it in a fine paste, and bake them or fry them, so done in the serving of them cast blaunch powder upon them.

THE GOOD HUSWIFES JEWELL, 1587

Individual Meat Pies with Cointreau Marmalade

SERVES 8

*E*LIZABETHAN STREET VENDORS sold little minced pies like these, as well as oyster pies, apples, and nuts, to theatergoers. The audience ate during the entire play and tossed cores, shells, and scraps onto the theater floor.

These tiny meat pies delicately flavored with orange liqueur are just as perfect now as then, for picnics or pre-theater nibbling.

8 ounces ground lamb, beef, or veal

$\frac{1}{2}$ teaspoon salt

$\frac{1}{4}$ teaspoon freshly milled black pepper

$\frac{1}{4}$ teaspoon freshly ground nutmeg

$\frac{1}{2}$ teaspoon ground mace

3 pitted dried plums, finely chopped

$\frac{1}{2}$ cup currants

$\frac{1}{4}$ cup freshly squeezed orange juice

$\frac{1}{2}$ recipe of Renaissance Dough (page 239)

$\frac{1}{4}$ cup Cointreau

$\frac{1}{2}$ cup thick-cut orange marmalade

1. Combine the meat, pepper, salt, nutmeg, mace, dried plums, currants, and orange juice in a bowl and refrigerate for at least 6 hours, or overnight. Remove the meat mixture from the refrigerator 1 hour before baking.

2. Preheat the oven to 450°F. Roll out the Renaissance Dough $\frac{1}{16}$ inch thick on a floured work surface. Cut twenty-four 3-inch circles from the dough. Press the dough circles into mini-muffin pans. Loosely fill each muffin cup with the meat mixture (about 1 tablespoon per pie) and bake for 15 minutes.

3. Bring the Cointreau to a boil in a small saucepan, stir in the marmalade, and cook until the marmalade is warm.

4. Spoon some of the marmalade mixture on top of each mince pie and serve.

Italian travel writers visiting England during this period noted disapprovingly that not only did the English eat inside theaters, but they also ate while strolling in the streets, a practice frowned upon in Italy.

But, not all visitors were critical. One German traveler wrote of the English, "They are more polite in Eating than the French, devouring less Bread, but more Meat, which they roast in Perfection." He also noted that when an Englishman saw a particularly attractive, well-groomed foreigner, he would say, "It is a Pity he is not an Englishman."

And I'll be sworn 'tis true: travelers ne'er did lie,
Though fools at home condemn 'em.
THE TEMPEST, 3.3

Salmon with Violets

SERVES 4

I know a bank where the wild thyme blows,
Where oxlips and the nodding violet grows . . .

A MIDSUMMER NIGHT'S DREAM, 2.1

THE BEAUTIFUL COLORS, the presentation, and the wonderful light flavors of this dish typify the sophistication of Elizabethan cuisine. Many types of edible flowers were used in cooking, both for their visual appeal and for their taste. Flowers were not set out onto the table in vases, but rather the dinner platters and the food itself were considered the decoration and were enhanced with flowers. Cookbooks of the time even list instructions on salads "for shewe only" with details on creating large elaborate "flowers" made of various cut vegetables and herbs.

2 tablespoons white wine vinegar

1 teaspoon sugar

1 tablespoon freshly squeezed lemon juice

¼ cup extra-virgin olive oil

Salt and freshly milled black pepper

1 large Vidalia onion, sliced paper-thin

1 salmon fillet, cut into 4 strips (about 12 ounces)

¾ cup edible violets

1. Place the vinegar, sugar, and lemon juice in a small bowl and slowly whisk in the olive oil. Season to taste with salt and pepper. Toss the onion in the vinaigrette and set aside.

2. Preheat the grill. Lightly coat the salmon with a little vinaigrette and cook for 3 to 4 minutes on each side, or until firm.

3. Place a mound of the onion in the center of each plate and top with a piece of salmon. Drizzle the remaining vinaigrette over the salmon and arrange the violets on the salmon and around the plate.

An other [Sallets for fish days]

Salmon cut long waies with slices of onyons upon it layd and upon that to cast Violets, Oyle and Vineger.

THE GOOD HUSWIFES JEWELL, 1587

Spring Pea Tortellini

SERVES 8 TO 10 (APPROXIMATELY 80 TORTELLINI)

> . . . and I remember the wooing of a peascod instead of her,
> from whom I took two cods and, giving her them again, said
> with weeping tears 'Wear these for my sake.'
>
> *AS YOU LIKE IT, 2.4*

PEASCODS, OR PEA PODS, usually gathered in springtime, were exchanged as a token of love. An old English proverb states, "Winter time for shoeing, peascod time for wooing." According to Elizabethans, if you tugged a pea pod off the vine and it stayed intact, it meant someone was in love with you.

If you don't want to make the tortellini, you can get almost the same taste combination by tossing one pound of cooked spaghetti with the pea mixture and sprinkling on the delicious and unusual Parmesan-cinnamon topping.

2 large eggs

3½ cups flour

½ cup white wine

1 small onion, minced

2 tablespoons extra-virgin olive oil

1 pound fresh shelled peas, parboiled (or frozen

     petite peas, thawed)

1 cup whole-milk ricotta cheese

1½ cups freshly grated Parmesan cheese

½ teaspoon freshly grated nutmeg

¼ teaspoon freshly milled black pepper

1 tablespoon granulated sugar

½ teaspoon ground cinnamon

1 tablespoon confectioners' sugar

2 quarts Renaissance Stock (page 240)

12 sweet pea flowers (optional)

1. Combine the eggs, flour, and wine in a large bowl and mix with a fork until the dough begins to come together. Knead the dough for 10 minutes, or until it feels velvety. Cover well with plastic wrap and set aside at room temperature for up to 3 hours.

2. Cook the onion and olive oil in a sauté pan over low heat for 10 minutes. Add the peas and cook for 1 minute. Let cool to room temperature and purée until smooth. Place the ricotta cheese, ½ cup of the Parmesan cheese, the nutmeg, and pepper in a large bowl. Add the pea purée and mix well.

3. Roll out one fourth of the dough at a time into a paper-thin sheet and cut out circles with a 3-inch ring cutter. Place a teaspoonful of the filling in the center of each pasta circle and fold in half, pinching the edges to form a tight seal. Pinch the two ends of each half circle together to form the tortellini. Repeat the process with the remaining dough. The tortellini can be placed on a floured baking sheet, covered in plastic wrap, and refrigerated for up to 4 hours.

4. Combine the remaining 1 cup Parmesan cheese, the granulated sugar, cinnamon, and confectioners' sugar in a small bowl.

5. Bring the Renaissance Stock to a boil in a large saucepan. Add the tortellini and cook for 2 to 3 minutes, or until they float. Remove from the stock with a slotted spoon and drain well.

6. Toss the tortellini in the Parmesan mixture and spoon onto the center of each plate. Arrange the sweet pea flowers over the tortellini and serve immediately.

ORIGINAL RECIPE:

Tortelleti, of green Pease, French Beans,
or any kind of Pulse green or dry

Take pease green or dry, French beans, or garden beans green or dry, boil them tender, and stamp them; strain them through a strainer, and put to them some fried onions chopped small, sugar, cinamon, cloves, pepper and nutmeg, some grated parmisan, or fat cheese, and some cheese curds stamped.

Then make paste, and make little pasties, boil them in broth, or as beforesaid, and serve them with sugar, cinamon, and grated cheese in a fine clean dish.

THE ACCOMPLISHT COOK, 1660

Crab with Pistachios and Pine Nuts

SERVES 4

ONE OF THE ORIGINAL garnishes suggested for this dish was buttery biscuits. For feasts given by the wealthy or noble, the pastry might have been shaped in the family crest or coat of arms. Interestingly, in 1596, Shakespeare officially registered his own family coat of arms. Demonstrating his love of word play, he selected a crest that featured a long spear, an obvious pun on his last name. For your own Shakespeare pun garnish with asparagus spears!

¼ cup pine nuts

¼ cup pistachios

6 ounces crabmeat, cleaned

¼ cup white wine

¼ teaspoon freshly grated nutmeg

1 large egg, beaten

¼ cup dried bread crumbs

1 tablespoon freshly squeezed lemon juice

2 tablespoons finely chopped flat-leaf parsley

⅛ teaspoon salt

2 blood oranges, peeled and sliced ¼ inch thick

1 teaspoon dark brown sugar

1 tablespoon unsalted butter, melted

Asparagus spears, blanched (optional)

1. Place the pine nuts and pistachios in a double layer of plastic bags and pound them a few times with a meat mallet. (They should still be fairly coarse.)

2. Combine the crabmeat, nuts, wine, nutmeg, egg, bread crumbs, lemon juice, parsley, and salt (omit salt if canned crab is used) until well mixed.

3. Preheat the broiler. Using a cookie scoop or a tablespoon, drop about 2 tablespoons of the crab mixture at a time onto a greased baking sheet and pat gently to form a dome shape. Broil for 6 minutes, or until light golden at the edges.

4. Place the orange slices on a baking sheet and sprinkle with brown sugar and butter. Broil for 1 minute, or until they just begin to brown.

5. Place 4 crab cakes in the center of each plate and arrange the orange slices around the plate. If using, garnish with asparagus spears.

Dried Plums with Wine and Ginger–Zest Crostini

SERVES 8 TO 10

Sir, she came in great with child; and longing, saving
your honour's reverence, for stewed prunes . . .

MEASURE FOR MEASURE, 2.1

*T*HIS SIXTEENTH-CENTURY recipe calls for the dried plums to be served in a tart as part of the first course. However, in another cookbook of the time, *L'Opera*, by Bartolomeo Scappi, published in Italy in 1570, a similar dried-plum mix is served on toast points as an appetizer, as suggested here.

The striking contrast of the ginger and lemon zest against the dark purple plums makes this unusual appetizer both beautiful and delicious.

1 cup red wine

2 tablespoons sugar

6 ounces pitted dried plums

1 2-inch cinnamon stick

1 loaf French baguette bread

2 tablespoons extra-virgin olive oil

Salt

2 tablespoons finely julienned fresh ginger

Zest of ½ lemon

1. Place the wine, sugar, dried plums, and cinnamon stick in a nonreactive saucepan. Simmer over medium heat for 30 minutes, or until the mixture is thickened. Remove the cinnamon stick and mash the dried plums with a fork.

2. Preheat the broiler. Cut the baguette into ¼-inch-thick slices and place on a baking sheet. Brush the slices with the olive oil and sprinkle lightly with salt. Toast under the broiler for 3 to 5 minutes, or until light golden brown.

3. Spread 1 tablespoon of the warm plum mixture on each toasted bread slice and sprinkle with the ginger and lemon zest.

To make a tartes of proines

Put your proines into a pot, and put in red wine or Claret wine, & a little ſaire water, stirre them nowe and then, and when they be boyled enough, put them into a bowle and strain them with sugar, synamon, and ginger.

THE GOOD HUSWIFES JEWELL, 1587

Damson plums were a favorite Elizabethan fruit and "eaten before dyner, be good to provoke a mans appetyde." They were also popular dried into prunes. It is unclear why, perhaps because they allegedly inflamed men's appetites, but stewed prunes were a favorite dish at Elizabethan brothels and also were a synonym for prostitutes. Shakespeare mentions prunes in that context in *King Henry IV, The Merry Wives of Windsor,* and *Measure for Measure.*

Prawns in Citrus Cream

*T*HE COMMON MAN ate prawns and shrimp simply prepared, just boiled and dipped in vinegar. Shell-fish were also appreciated by the upper classes, and this more elegant dish combining prawns and succulent oysters was designed with them in mind.

1 lemon

1 orange

2 tablespoons whole-wheat flour

Salt and freshly milled black pepper

2 tablespoons canola oil

4 medium-large oysters, shelled

1 teaspoon butter, unsalted

12 prawns (or shrimp), peeled and deveined

¼ cup cream

4 bay leaves

1. Zest the lemon and set aside the zest. Remove the remaining white pith and cut the lemon into ¼-inch-thick slices.

2. Zest the orange and set aside the zest. Remove the remaining white pith and cut the orange into ¼-inch-thick slices.

3. Place the flour in a small bowl and season with salt and pepper. Heat the oil in a small sauté pan over medium heat. Dredge the oysters in the flour and cook for 2 minutes on each side, or until golden brown. Remove from the pan and drain on paper towels. Wipe out the pan. Melt the butter in the pan, add the prawns, and cook for 3 minutes on each side, or until pink and firm. Add the lemon zest, orange zest, and cream and cook until just warm.

4. Place shrimp in the center of a serving platter and arrange the oysters around them. Spoon the sauce over the shrimp and oysters. Alternate the orange and lemon slices with the bay leaves around the outside of the serving platter.

To fry Oysters

Take two quarts of great Oysters being parboil'd in their own liquor, and washed in warm water, bread them, dry them, and, flour them, fry them in clarified butter crisp and white, then have butter'd prawns or shrimps, butter'd with cream and sweet butter, lay them in the bottom of a clean dish, and lay the fryed oysters round about them, run them over with beaten butter, juyce of oranges, bay-leaves stuck round the Oysters, and slices of oranges or lemons.

THE ACCOMPLISHT COOK, 1660

In this original recipe the sauce is thickened with "beaten butter" until emulsified. The Elizabethans also thickened their sauces with egg yolks or ground almonds. A curious fact surfaces in reading these Elizabethan cookbooks. The English did not thicken their sauces with flour. According to some scholars, it was actually a French chef, François Pierre de la Varenne, who first used that method in his 1661 cookbook, *Le Cuisinier François.* The English chefs of the time clearly shunned La Varenne's method of thickening, and it does not enter into English cookery books for at least fifty years. Similarly, the French rejected the Elizabethan technique of thickening a stock or sauce at the end by whisking in cold butter, a practice that today is highly associated with French cuisine. After visiting France in 1617, travel writer Frayn Moryson noted that the French used very little butter, commenting further, "nor have I tasted there any good Butter."

Herb Tart

SERVES 6

*I*N ELIZABETHAN ENGLAND the word *herb* meant any edible leafy vegetables, herbs, root vegetable tops, or salad lettuces. It is this assortment of baby greens that adds distinctive flavor and texture to this lovely tart. The author calls for the top crust to be "cut with pretie worke" or decorative cutout designs, but I like the way the pie looks without a top crust.

½ recipe of Renaissance Dough (page 239)

2 medium onions, finely chopped

2 tablespoons extra-virgin olive oil

1½ tablespoons minced fresh ginger

1 garlic clove, minced

1½ pounds assorted baby greens, finely chopped
(such as beet leaves, spinach, and endive)

1 cup finely chopped assorted herbs (such as flat-
leaf parsley, mint, thyme, and basil)

1 cup grated semisoft cheese

1 large egg, beaten

½ cup currants

1 teaspoon sugar

Salt and freshly milled black pepper

1. Roll out the Renaissance Dough ⅛ inch thick on a floured work surface. Press the dough into a 9-inch pie pan. Refrigerate the piecrust for 20 minutes.

2. Preheat the oven to 375°F. Bake the crust for 5 minutes.

3. Place the onions and olive oil in a large sauté pan and cook over low heat for 10 minutes. Add the ginger and garlic and cook for 1 minute. Raise the burner to high heat, add the greens and herbs, and cook for 1 minute, or until just wilted. Remove the pan from the heat, add the cheese, egg, currants, and sugar,

and mix well. Season to taste with salt and pepper. Pour the mixture into the pie shell and bake for 30 minutes, or until the crust is golden brown.

This recipe was for "fish days," one of more than 153 days per year when meat consumption was prohibited. The Church of England initially imposed fast days for spiritual and moral discipline because meat was thought to provoke carnal thoughts and incite passions. However, fish consumption was also encouraged to spark the shipbuilding industry and provide England with trained sailors for possible future military defense, as a good navy was clearly an essential defense for an island nation.

Oysters on Spinach with Capers

SERVES 4

> 'Good friend,' quoth he,
> 'Say, the firm Roman to great Egypt sends
> This treasure of an oyster . . .'
>
> *ANTONY AND CLEOPATRA, 1.5*

THIS LINE FROM *Antony and Cleopatra* suggests that Shakespeare was familiar with food history. It was indeed the Romans who first cultivated oysters near Naples in 100 B.C. and introduced them into Egypt and other areas.

The "faggot of sweet herbs" referred to in the original is a tied bundle of herbs, or bouquet garni. According to English dietary books, bouquet garni was much healthier than minced herbs, "the grose binding together and seething of herbes in brothes and pottage, be more holesomer then the fyne choppynge of them."

Mace, the outer husk of nutmeg, often called for in Elizabethan recipes, is available in most supermarkets. Mace adds a lovely touch to this oyster dish and, in fact, has become one of my favorite new spices. I use it in recipes that call for nutmeg, but I especially like it with fish.

1 loaf French baguette bread, cut in
 $\frac{1}{2}$-inch-thick slices

1 tablespoon extra-virgin olive oil

3 sprigs of flat-leaf parsley

2 endive leaves

3 sprigs of mint

2 tablespoons butter

12 large oysters, shelled, liquid reserved

2 tablespoons small capers, rinsed and drained

$\frac{1}{4}$ teaspoon ground mace

$\frac{1}{4}$ teaspoon ground marjoram

$\frac{1}{4}$ teaspoon dried thyme

$\frac{1}{4}$ teaspoon salt

8 ounces baby spinach

2 lemons, thinly sliced

1. Preheat the broiler. Brush the bread slices with the olive oil and broil for 2 to 3 minutes, or until lightly browned.

2. Tie together the parsley, endive, and mint with kitchen string. Melt the butter in a frying pan over medium heat. Add the oysters, the reserved oyster liquid, the capers, mace, marjoram, thyme, salt, and the herb bundle to the pan. Cover and cook for 1 minute. Turn over the oysters and cook for 1 minute. Remove the oysters from the pan with a slotted spoon and place in a warm dish. Add the spinach to the pan, cover, and cook for 1 minute, or until just wilted. Remove and discard the herb bundle.

3. Place a heaping tablespoon of spinach in the center of each plate and top with 3 oysters. Spoon the caper sauce over the oysters and arrange the lemon slices around the plate. Serve the French bread slices on the side.

ORIGINAL RECIPE:

Other ways [to make oyster pottage]

Take a quart of great oysters, parboil them in their own liquor, and stew them in a pipkin with some capers, large mace, a faggot of sweet herbs, salt, and butter, being finely stewed, serve them on slices of dried French bread, round the oysters slic't lemon, and on the pottage boil'd spinach, minced, and buttered, but first pour on the broth.

THE ACCOMPLISHT COOK, 1660

Off goes his bonnet to an oyster-wench . . .
KING RICHARD II, 1.4

Oysters were inexpensive and plentiful in England during Shakespeare's day. Mountains of oyster shells have been uncovered at excavation sites throughout London. Street vendors, such as Shakespeare's "oyster-wench," sold oysters to theatergoers as they entered the Globe to see a play. A typical food at taverns and inns, oysters were enjoyed pickled, roasted, broiled, fried, or raw with vinegar and onions.

Pâté with Dates and Homemade Nutmeg Mustard

SERVES 4

ATÉ WAS DEVELOPED in Ancient Greece after Sparta's king received a gift of fattened geese from Egypt. It was the English, however, who created this delicious combination of liver, wine, and sweet dried currants. The original was simmered in a tied cloth similar to an English pudding, but this modern version is much simpler to prepare and more attractive. The nutmeg mustard can be adjusted to suit your taste by adding more or less honey.

8 ounces veal liver, thinly sliced

½ cup milk

2 ounces pancetta, finely chopped

3 large shallots, minced

¼ cup cream

2 tablespoons butter, at room temperature

¼ teaspoon salt

¼ cup currants

6 dates, pitted and diced

2 teaspoons dried mustard

½ teaspoon freshly ground nutmeg

1 tablespoon honey

2 tablespoons sugar

1 tablespoon white wine

1 tablespoon white wine vinegar

1 loaf French baguette bread, thinly sliced

2 tablespoons extra-virgin olive oil

1. Soak the liver in the milk overnight.
2. Cook the pancetta in a large sauté pan over medium-low heat for 5 minutes, or until some of the fat is released. Add the shallots and cook over low heat for 4 minutes. Add the drained liver and cook for 2 to 3 minutes, or until the liver is still a little pink inside. Remove the pan from the heat and cool to room temperature.

3. Place the liver mixture in a food processor and purée until it forms a smooth paste. Add the cream, butter, salt, currants, and dates and purée until smooth. Place the mixture in individual ramekins and refrigerate until ready to serve.

4. Combine the mustard, nutmeg, honey, sugar, white wine, and vinegar in a small bowl.

5. Preheat the broiler. Place the bread slices on a baking sheet and brush with the olive oil. Toast the bread under the broiler for 3 to 5 minutes, or until light golden brown.

6. Place a ramekin of pâté on each plate. Place a dollop of mustard alongside the ramekin and arrange the toasted bread around the plate.

ORIGINAL RECIPE:

To make liver Puddings

Take a good hogs, calves, or lambs liver, and boil it: being cold, mince it very small, or grate it, and searce it through a meal-sieve or cullender, put to it some grated manchet [white bread rolls], two penny loaves, some three pints of cream, four eggs, cloves, mace, currans, salt, dates, sugar, cinamon, ginger, nutmegs, one pound of beef-suet minced very small: being mixt all together, fill a wet napkin, and bind it in fashion of a ball, and serve it with beaten butter and sugar being boil'd.

THE ACCOMPLISHT COOK, 1660

Renaissance Rice Balls

*R*ICE BALLS like these, today known as "arancine," or little oranges, are still made in many parts of Italy. During the Renaissance these savory balls would have been colored purple or yellow with dried edible flower petals or saffron. This dish can be easily re-created using food coloring to produce the different colored balls. Of course, they are delicious without the coloring!

1 pound Italian rice (such as arborio)

⅓ cup cream

1 large egg, beaten

1 cup grated caciocavallo cheese

2 tablespoons sugar

Yellow food coloring (optional)

Purple food coloring (optional)

½ cup flour or dried bread crumbs

¾ cup vegetable oil

1. Cook the rice according to the package directions. Combine the cooked rice, cream, egg, cheese, and sugar in a large bowl. Cover and refrigerate until thoroughly chilled, or up to 2 days.

2. If desired, divide the rice into 3 equal portions. Using the food coloring, color 1 portion bright yellow, 1 portion purple, and leave the remaining portion white.

3. Form each of the portions of rice into 1-inch-diameter balls.

4. Place the flour or bread crumbs on a flat plate. Heat 3 to 4 tablespoons of oil in a skillet over medium-high heat. Lightly roll 1 color of the rice balls in the flour or bread crumbs. Cook, turning occasionally, until completely browned on all sides. Remove the rice balls from the pan and drain on paper towels. Discard the oil in the pan, wipe it clean, and repeat the process with the remaining rice balls.

Veal with Glazed Grapes on Saffron Toast

SERVES 4

> . . . I must have saffron to colour the warden pies; mace; dates?—
> none, that's out of my note; nutmegs, seven; a race or two of ginger,
> but that I may beg; four pound of prunes, and as many of
> raisins o' the sun.
>
> *THE WINTER'S TALE, 4.3*

*D*URING THE Middle Ages and into Elizabethan times, foods such as Shakespeare's pear, or "warden" pie, were often colored yellow with saffron or sandalwood. Other dishes were colored green with parsley or spinach juice, white with ground almonds, rice, or milk, and black with prunes. In this recipe the baguettes are brushed with saffron-infused oil to give a hint of color and flavor.

2½ cups dessert wine

2 tablespoons extra-virgin olive oil

Pinch of saffron

8 ounces ground veal

2 tablespoons minced onion

2 tablespoons dried bread crumbs

2 teaspoons chopped flat-leaf parsley

1 large egg yolk

Salt and freshly milled black pepper

16 ¼-inch-thick slices French baguette bread

½ cup grapes, quartered (green, red, or black)

1. Place the wine in a small saucepan and simmer over medium-low heat for 1 hour, or until reduced to about ¼ cup. Set aside.

2. Combine the olive oil and saffron in a small bowl and let it steep for 30 minutes.

3. Place the veal, onion, bread crumbs, parsley, and egg yolk in a small bowl. Season with salt and pepper and mix until combined. Divide the mixture into 16 portions and roll into balls. Form each ball into an oval patty about ¼ inch thick. Cook the patties in a large nonstick sauté pan over medium-low heat for 2 to 3 minutes on each side, or until done.

4. Preheat the oven to 350°F. Place the bread slices on a baking sheet and brush with the saffron mixture. Bake for 8 to 10 minutes, or until light golden brown.

5. Place 4 slices of bread in the center of each plate. Add the grapes to the reduced wine and stir until coated. Dip each of the veal patties into the glaze and place one on each of the bread slices. Arrange the grape quarters on top of the veal and drizzle with the remaining glaze.

Saffron, originally imported from Greece, Sicily, and Asia Minor, was the most expensive spice available in Shakespeare's day. England began small-scale cultivation of saffron in the 1400s, but it was mainly imported from Spain. Saffron was prized for its subtle flavor and the golden color it imparts. Thought to strengthen the heart, it was listed in many remedies as well as used in cooking and to flavor wines.

Pottage: Soups and Stews

Asses, fools, dolts! chaff and bran, chaff and bran!

porridge after meat!

TROILUS AND CRESSIDA, 1.2

. . . .

The English ate soup, or porridge as they called it, with the first course and considered it absurd to serve it following the meat course. However, for the rest of Europe, pottage accompanied the second or third course of roast meats.

In general, pottage and broth were more popular in England than in the warmer Mediterranean countries. As one traveler of the time noted, "Potage is nat so moch used in all Crystendom as it is used in England."

The Oxford-trained Elizabethan physician Thomas Cogan expressed frustration with his countrymen who, after traveling to the Continent, would adopt unhealthy foreign dining customs and, "despising the olde order of England, would not begin his meales with potage. . . . But," he wrote, "wise Englishmen I trust will use the old English fashion still."

Velvet Soup with Grapes

SERVES 4

*T*HE ORIGINAL INSTRUCTIONS for this delicious soup are a little imprecise, with vague but charming advice such as "take heede you boyle them not too much, nor yet too little" and "stir them a good while." However, the original recipe is very clear on the simple technique of slowly adding egg yolks to obtain a velvety-smooth and rich broth. The sweet flavor of the soup is perfectly complemented by the tang of the grapes.

8 green grapes, quartered

8 black grapes, quartered

8 ounces cooked chicken (or lamb), shredded

4 large egg yolks

2 cups Renaissance Stock (page 240)

2 tablespoons verjuice (available at gourmet
    grocers, verjuice is a light vinegar made from
    unripened grapes, or use any fruit vinegar)

1/4 teaspoon dried savory

1/4 teaspoon dried thyme

1/4 teaspoon dried rosemary

1/4 teaspoon dried marjoram

2 tablespoons cold butter, cut into 8 cubes

1. Combine the green and black grapes and the meat in a small bowl. Let stand for 1 hour or heat for 1 to 2 minutes in a small saucepan to bring to room temperature.

2. Whisk 1 egg yolk and 1/2 cup of the Renaissance Stock in a double boiler over gently boiling water until creamy. Add another egg yolk and 1/2 cup of stock and whisk until creamy. Repeat until all stock and egg yolks are used and the soup is warm. Whisk in the verjuice, savory, thyme, rosemary, and marjoram. Whisk in the butter and remove from the heat. Do not allow the soup to boil, or it will curdle.

3. Ladle the soup into 4 bowls. Arrange the chicken and grapes in the center of each bowl.

"Pears" in Broth

*T*HIS IMPRESSIVE DISH was designed with a feast in mind. The meatballs, with their sage-leaf stems, resemble tiny speckled pears. Since ancient times chefs have taken pleasure in delighting diners with meat, marzipan, and dough sculptures of animals, fruits, flowers, and even the likenesses of special guests.

8 ounces ground veal or pork

¼ cup dried whole-wheat bread crumbs

1 large egg

1 tablespoon finely chopped thyme

2 tablespoons finely chopped flat-leaf parsley

½ teaspoon salt

Pinch of ground cloves

12 small green seedless grapes

12 sage leaves, with stems

1½ quarts Renaissance Stock, warm (page 240)

Pinch of saffron threads

1. Combine the veal, bread crumbs, egg, thyme, parsley, salt, and cloves in a bowl. Divide the mixture into 12 equal portions. Wrap each portion of meat around a grape and form a pear shape. Refrigerate until ready to cook.

2. Preheat the broiler. Place the pears upright on a well-greased pan and broil 4 to 5 inches from the flame for 4 minutes, or until done. Using a toothpick, gently imbed a sage leaf into the top of each pear.

3. Carefully place 2 pears in each serving bowl and ladle the Renaissance Stock with saffron threads around the pears.

Fish Bisque with Chestnuts and Artichokes

SERVES 6

*T*HIS FRENCH RECIPE was referred to as "Bisk" by the Elizabethan chef who misspelled *bisque*. The "corbolion" he mentions also derives from French for "court bouillon," a mix of water, white wine, vinegar, and herbs used for cooking fish. The word *jacks*, however, was the English term for pike and was also the English nickname for sailors.

Although odd spellings and new words attracted me to this original recipe, it was the chestnut and fish pairing that inspired me to cook it. Chestnuts, mostly relegated to my Thanksgiving stuffing, have now become a standard ingredient in soups and stews.

2 onions, minced

2 celery stalks, minced

1 tablespoon extra-virgin olive oil

1 tablespoon butter

1 cup white wine

One 8-ounce sea bass fillet, cut into 1-inch cubes

One 8-ounce cod fillet, cut into 1-inch cubes

$\frac{1}{8}$ teaspoon dried thyme

$\frac{1}{8}$ teaspoon dried savory

$\frac{1}{8}$ teaspoon dried marjoram

$\frac{1}{8}$ teaspoon dried rosemary

2 whole bay leaves

1 cup finely chopped assorted fresh greens (such
     as flat-leaf parsley, baby spinach, or endive)

1 cup blanched chestnuts, diced

4 artichoke bottoms, cooked and diced

4 prawns, shell on

$\frac{1}{4}$ cup coarsely chopped pistachios, lightly toasted

1. Sauté the onions and celery in the olive oil and butter in a large saucepan over low heat for 10 minutes. Add 3 cups of water and the wine and bring to a boil. Add the sea bass, cod, thyme, savory, marjoram, rosemary, bay leaves, greens, chestnuts, and artichoke bottoms and reduce the heat to medium-low. Simmer for 10 minutes, stirring every 2 or 3 minutes to help break apart the fish. Add the prawns and simmer for 5 minutes. Remove the prawns, peel, and finely dice.

2. Ladle the soup into the bowls and top with the diced prawns. Sprinkle the chopped pistachios over the soup and serve immediately.

Oyster Stew

SERVES 4

Why, then the world's mine oyster,
Which I with sword will open.

THE MERRY WIVES OF WINDSOR, 2.2

THE ORIGINAL RECIPE calls for "slic't nutmeg," a sophisticated touch to add flavor to a dish. Nutmeg, one of the most common spices in Elizabethan recipes, became so popular that eighteenth- and nineteenth-century ladies and gentlemen carried small personal silver nutmeg graters with them to dinner parties.

1 small red onion, diced

1 tablespoon butter

1 cup white wine

12 small oysters, liquid reserved

1 cup milk

½ teaspoon freshly ground nutmeg

Salt

½ teaspoon freshly milled pink peppercorns

½ cup coarsely cut toasted bread

1. Sauté the onion and butter in a saucepan over medium-low heat for 10 minutes, or until translucent. Add the wine and bring to a boil. Reduce to low heat, add the oysters and their liquid, and cook for 4 minutes. Add the milk, nutmeg, and salt and cook for 3 minutes.

2. Ladle the stew into the serving bowl and top with the pink peppercorns and toasted bread.

Seafood Soup with Rosemary Croutons

*T*HIS RECIPE caught my attention with its instructions to use "a good many of sliced Onyons," always a sign to me of a tasty soup to come. The currants contribute a light sweetness and the simple-to-make rosemary croutons top it off perfectly.

In Shakespeare's time to ensure fresh fish for meals, noblemen built artificial ponds on their estates stocked and maintained by full-time fishermen. The middle classes had to make do with a rain barrel outside the kitchen door to keep their catch fresh.

1 large onion, diced

2 tablespoons butter

8 ounces carp, skinned and diced

½ teaspoon dried rosemary

½ teaspoon dried parsley

½ teaspoon dried thyme

½ teaspoon dried marjoram

½ cup white wine

¼ cup currants

¼ teaspoon ground mace

1 tablespoon sugar

Salt and freshly milled black pepper

1 teaspoon dried rosemary leaves

6 slices French bread, about ¼ inch thick

1. Sauté the onion in 1 tablespoon of the butter in a saucepan over medium heat for 10 minutes, or until golden. Add 4 cups of water, the carp, rosemary, parsley, thyme, and marjoram and simmer for 5 minutes. Add the wine, currants, mace, and sugar, reduce to low heat, and simmer for 15 minutes. Season to taste with salt and pepper.

2. Preheat the broiler. Melt the remaining 1 tablespoon of butter and stir in the rosemary leaves. Brush the butter mixture on the bread slices and broil for 1 to 2 minutes, or until golden brown. Roughly cut the bread slices into small croutons.

3. Ladle the soup into 4 bowls and sprinkle with the croutons.

Almond-Orange Broth

A LMONDS, A FAVORITE ingredient throughout Shakespeare's time, were ground and mixed with water as a substitute for cow's milk on days when animal products were prohibited. Here, the subtle flavors of the dried fruits and almonds combine with the broth to make this soup light, aromatic, and exceptionally delicious.

1 quart Renaissance Stock (page 240)

¼ teaspoon dried rosemary

¼ teaspoon dried thyme

¼ teaspoon dried hyssop

¼ teaspoon dried marjoram

½ teaspoon ground mace

½ teaspoon ground ginger

1 tablespoon sugar

½ cup finely ground blanched almonds

1 teaspoon rose water

½ cup freshly squeezed orange juice

Zest of 1 orange

¼ cup sliced almonds

1. Combine the Renaissance Stock, rosemary, thyme, hyssop, marjoram, mace, ginger, sugar, and ground almonds in a saucepan and simmer for 20 minutes. Remove from the heat and add the rose water and orange juice. Purée until smooth. Warm the soup just prior to serving.

2. Ladle the soup into 4 bowls and top with the orange zest and sliced almonds.

Blanching, from the French word *blanc* for white, means to remove the bitter skins, and the technique is noted as far back as 1390 in the *Forme of Curie.* The word *almond* also comes from the Old French *almande,* and even *jordan,* a type of almond, comes from the French *jardin,* or garden.

Cauliflower Chowder

SERVES 4 TO 6

*V*ERJUICE, THE JUICE of unripe grapes now available in most gourmet grocers, adds a lovely touch to this velvety, mild chowder. If you plan on making the soup ahead, reserve some of the florets and roast them just before serving so they are crisp. In fact, these slow-roasted cauliflower "croutons" are so irresistibly delicious you might want to buy two heads of cauliflower and make extra!

1 head of cauliflower

Salt

1 large onion, diced

2 tablespoons butter

3½ cups Renaissance Stock (page 240)

½ cup sweet sherry

3 whole mace blades (or ⅛ teaspoon ground mace)

1 cup milk

Freshly milled black pepper

1 tablespoon verjuice

1 teaspoon lemon zest

1. Preheat the oven to 250°F. Remove 1 cup of small florets from the cauliflower for the "croutons." Coarsely chop the remainder and reserve. Sprinkle salt on a nonstick baking pan, add the cup of florets, and bake for 1 hour, or until deep brown and dry. Remove from the pan and discard the salt.

2. Cook the onion in the butter in a large saucepan over medium-low heat for 10 minutes. Add the reserved chopped cauliflower and cook for 5 minutes. Add the Renaissance Stock, sherry, and mace and simmer for 20 minutes. Remove the mace and purée the cauliflower mixture until smooth. Add the milk and simmer over low heat, stirring frequently, for 10 minutes. (Use low heat, or the soup will scorch and separate.) Season to taste with salt and pepper.

3. Ladle the soup into individual bowls and drizzle with a few drops of verjuice. Sprinkle the cauliflower "croutons" and lemon zest over the soup.

Italian Pea Pottage

SERVES 8 TO 10

*P*EASE PORRIDGE in the pot, nine days old" fairly well summarizes the technique of stew preparation in Shakespeare's day. A thick soup would have been left cooking for days at a time, with new vegetables, stock, and bits of leftover meat continually added. This Italian version contains rich duck meat, a delicious and unusual addition to pea soup.

2 slices thick-cut smoked bacon

1 large red onion, diced

1 quart Renaissance Stock (page 240)

1 pound dried green split peas, rinsed

½ teaspoon freshly milled black pepper

1 tablespoon salt

1 tablespoon coarsely crushed aniseed

1 cup finely chopped flat-leaf parsley

1 cup shredded smoked duck breast

Cook the bacon in a large saucepan over medium heat for 7 to 10 minutes, or until crisp. Remove the bacon from the pan, cut into small pieces, and set aside. Add the onion to the pan and cook for 10 minutes, or until golden brown. Add the Renaissance Stock, peas, bacon pieces, and 2 cups of water, and simmer for 1 hour, skimming away any impurities that rise to the top. Add the pepper, salt, and aniseed and simmer for 15 minutes. Remove from the heat, stir in the parsley and duck, and serve immediately.

ORIGINAL RECIPE:

Pottage in the Italian Fashion

Boil green pease with some strong broth, and interlarded bacon cut into slices; the
pease being boiled, put to them some chopped parsley, pepper, anniseed, and strain
some of the pease to thicken the broth; give it a walm [warm it] and serve it on sippets,
with boiled chickens, pigeons, kids, or lambs-heads, mutton, duck, mallard, or any
poultry. Sometimes for variety you may thicken the broth with eggs.

THE ACCOMPLISHT COOK, 1660

Lamb with Sorrel

*T*HIS SOUP, originally listed as a fertility enhancer, "to strengthen the seed of man or woman," contained ingredients then thought to be aphrodisiacs. Shakespeare almost certainly knew of this soup, as the recipe is taken from a 1596 cookbook found in old inventories from Stratford-upon-Avon.

1 quart Renaissance Stock (page 240)

½ cup diced sweet potato

½ cup sorrel or baby spinach, finely julienned

½ cup finely sliced endive

3 ounces cooked lamb

Salt and freshly milled black pepper

Edible violets (optional)

1. Bring the Renaissance Stock to a simmer over medium-low heat. Add the sweet potato and simmer for 15 minutes, or until tender. Remove from the heat, add the sorrel, endive, and lamb, and season to taste with salt and pepper.

2. Top the soup with a few violets, if desired.

ORIGINAL RECIPE:

To strengthen the seed of man or woman

Take succory, endive, plantin, violet flowers and the leaves, clary, sorrel, or each a handful, with a piece of Mutton, make a good broth, and to eat it evening and morning is special good.

THE TREASURIE OF HIDDEN SECRETS, COMONLIE CALLED THE GOOD HUSWIVES CLOSET OF PROVISIONS, 1633 EDITION OF THE 1596 BOOK

Broth has long been believed to be healthful, and almost every culture seems to have its own version of that universal remedy, chicken soup. In *The Treasurie of Hidden Secrets,* another soup recipe claims to help predict a woman's fertility. Apparently, if the woman developed a stomachache after drinking the rabbit stew broth, she was deemed able to conceive. Elizabethan cookbooks contained other tests, remedies, and advice on fertility. One, which claimed to be able to make a "barren woman" bear children, included an elaborate recipe recommended to be taken daily, and the recipe ended with the additional advice that "it shall profit and helpe very much, having in the meantime the company of a man!"

Portuguese Renaissance Soup

SERVES 8

A man may break a word with you, sir, and
words are but wind,
Ay, and break it in your face, so he break it not behind.

THE COMEDY OF ERRORS, 3.1

*T*HE WORD *farts*, as used in the original recipe that inspired this soup, dates back to 1250 and, besides the expected definition of breaking wind, also meant light puff pastry. The English, who traded heavily with Portugal for wine, lemons, oranges, salt, and honey, were very familiar with Portuguese dishes such as this soup of light meat dumplings in broth.

8 ounces ground lamb

2 large eggs

½ cup cream

⅛ teaspoon ground cloves

½ teaspoon salt

Dash of freshly milled black pepper

½ teaspoon ground mace

5 pitted dates, finely chopped

¾ cup currants

1½ quarts Renaissance Stock, hot (page 240)

1. Purée the lamb, eggs, cream, cloves, salt, pepper, mace, dates, and ½ cup of the currants in a food processor until it forms a paste. Refrigerate for at least 1 hour.

2. Bring a saucepan of water to a slow simmer. Using 2 spoons, form ¾ teaspoon of the meat into an olive shape. Repeat with the remaining meat. Carefully place a few meatballs at a time into the water and simmer for 4 or 5 minutes, turning occasionally, until they are cooked on all sides. Remove with a slotted spoon and repeat until all the meatballs are cooked.

3. Place some of the meatballs in the bottom of each bowl. Gently ladle the Renaissance Stock into the bowl, being careful not to pour the stock directly on the meatballs. Sprinkle the remaining ¼ cup of currants around the stock.

How to make Farts of Portingale

Take a peece of a leg of Mutton, mince it smal and season it with cloves, Mace, pepper and salt, and Dates minced with currans: then roll it into round rolles, and so into little balles, and so boyle them in a little beefe broth and so serve them foorth.

THE GOOD HUSWIVES HANDMAIDE FOR COOKERIE IN HER KITCHIN, 1588

"Olepotrige" Stew from Renaissance Spain

SERVES 10

*A*CCORDING TO the 1615 recipe, this stew was considered "the onely principall dish of boild meate which is esteemed in al Spaine," where it was called *olla podrida*. *Olla* was the Spanish for cooking pot and *podrida* meant a spiced stew of various meats. Olla podrida was even mentioned by Cervantes in *Don Quixote*. It was apparently very popular in England, too, as it was included in several cookbooks of the time.

Don't let the length of the ingredient list prevent you from trying this tasty and easy-to-prepare dish. It goes together with a minimum of fuss and can simmer for hours unattended. The original recipe calls for even more ingredients, and lists over fifteen different meats.

1 tablespoon extra-virgin olive oil

8 ounces beef stew meat, cubed

3 ounces lamb, cubed

6 ounces pork, cubed

6 ounces veal, cubed

6 ounces boneless, skinless chicken breasts, cubed

2 large onions, diced

1 sweet potato, peeled and diced

1 turnip, peeled and diced

1 parsnip, peeled and diced

5 scallions, cut into 1-inch pieces

2 cups finely chopped assorted greens (such as
      spinach, endive, chicory, and parsley)

½ teaspoon dried thyme

1 teaspoon dried hyssop (optional)

½ teaspoon dried marjoram

1 tablespoon grated fresh ginger

½ teaspoon freshly ground nutmeg

4 whole cloves

1 teaspoon salt

½ cup currants

½ cup pitted and chopped dried plums

2 tablespoons verjuice

Salt and freshly milled black pepper

2 tablespoons coarsely chopped flat-leaf parsley,

　　for garnish

1. Heat the olive oil in a heavy-bottomed pot and add the beef, lamb, pork, veal, and chicken. Cook, stirring frequently, for 10 minutes, or until all the meat is browned. Remove the meat from the pot, add the onions, and cook over low heat for 10 minutes, or until soft. Increase the heat to medium-high and add 4 cups of water to the pot, scraping loose any drippings. Bring to a boil and add the meat, half of the sweet potato, half of the turnip, half of the parsnip, the scallions, greens, thyme, hyssop, marjoram, ginger, nutmeg, cloves, and salt. Cover and cook over medium-low heat for 1½ hours, stirring occasionally.

2. Add the currants, dried plums, and the remaining sweet potato, turnip, and parsnip and cook for 30 minutes. Add the verjuice and season to taste with salt and pepper.

3. Ladle the stew into shallow bowls and garnish with the chopped parsley.

The original recipe refers to the serving platter as a "charger," from the Old French for something used for loading. Another term for a dish or platter then was *trencher,* from the French *trancher,* to slice. Both terms originate in the Middle Ages when there were no plates. Instead, stale bread was sliced and meat and other food was placed on it. The used bread was then given to the poor or to livestock. The word *trencher,* however, remained the term for dishes even later when they were made of wood or other materials.

Beef Stew with Chestnuts and Onions

SERVES 4

*C*ASH," THE ORIGINAL title for this recipe, comes from *hacher*, French for chop. The French influence on English cooking is seen in this dish with its slow simmering of meat, wine, and herbs. The chestnuts are a wonderful natural thickener and add sweetness to this family-pleasing dish.

1 pound beef stew meat, cubed

¼ cup extra-virgin olive oil

2 large onions, sliced

1 quart Renaissance Stock (page 240)

1 cup red wine

¼ teaspoon freshly ground nutmeg

¼ teaspoon ground cloves

8 ounces chestnuts, roasted

4 ½-inch-thick slices French bread

1 tablespoon chopped flat-leaf parsley

1. Sear the stew meat in 2 tablespoons of the olive oil in a large saucepan over medium-high heat for 10 minutes, or until browned on all sides. Add one of the onions, the Renaissance Stock, wine, nutmeg, cloves, and half of the chestnuts to the pan and reduce heat to medium-low. Simmer for 2 hours, covered, stirring occasionally. Add the remaining onion and cook for 45 minutes. Add the remaining chestnuts and cook for 15 minutes.

2. Preheat the oven to 350°F. Place the bread slices on a baking sheet, brush on the remaining olive oil, and sprinkle with the parsley. Bake for 8 to 10 minutes, or until golden brown.

3. Ladle the stew into 4 bowls and top each bowl with a slice of the toasted bread.

To Make all manner of Hashes, First of raw Beef

Mince it very small with some Beef-suet or lard, some sweet herbs, pepper, salt, some cloves, and mace, blanched chestnuts, or almonds blanched, and put in whole, some nutmeg, and a whole onion or two, and stew it finely in a pipkin with some strong broth the space of two hours, put a little claret to it, and serve it on sippets finely carved, with some grapes or lemon in it also, or barberries, and blow off the fat.

THE ACCOMPLISHT COOK, 1660

CHAPTER THREE

CARROT AND SHRIMP SALAD

RENAISSANCE GARDEN

SPRING LETTUCE WITH CHIVE FLOWERS

ENDIVE TOPPED WITH PERIWINKLES

WINTER SALAD WITH RAISIN AND CAPER VINAIGRETTE

WATERCRESS WITH ROASTED PARSNIPS

MEDITERRANEAN ORANGE AND CAPER SALAD

SALLET OF LEMMONS

GRILLED TUNA WITH CARROTS AND SWEET ONIONS

WATERCRESS SALAD WITH SHERRY PEARS

Sallet

. . . .

This passage refers to the Renaissance belief that lettuces are "cooling" to the system. The theory that all foods possess some degree of hot, cold, dry, and moist originated in ancient Greece with the philosopher Aristotle and with the father of medicine, Hippocrates.

Combining certain foods was thought to be especially healthful, and balancing foods by pairing them with their complements was seen as particularly important. In fact, the classic salad of lettuce with oil and vinegar comes from that medical model. The so-called "cool and moist" lettuce was balanced by the oil ("hot and dry") and vinegar ("cool and dry").

Carrot and Shrimp Salad

SERVES 4

*T*HE SHREDDED CARROTS in the original recipe were arranged in the shape of a fleur-de-lis with the shrimp placed on the inside of the flower to form its center. In this modern version I cook the shrimp in carrot juice for added carrot flavor and sweetness.

8 ounces medium shrimp, peeled and deveined

½ cup carrot juice

1 tablespoon freshly squeezed lemon juice

2 tablespoons sherry vinegar

¼ cup extra-virgin olive oil

Salt and freshly milled black pepper

3 large carrots

Zest of ½ lemon

8 lemon wedges

1. Marinate the shrimp in 6 tablespoons of the carrot juice and the lemon juice for 1 hour. Place the shrimp and the marinade in a small saucepan and bring to a simmer over low heat. Cook for 3 to 5 minutes, or until just done. Drain the shrimp, mince, and refrigerate for 30 minutes, or until chilled.

2. Place the vinegar in a small bowl and slowly whisk in the olive oil. Season to taste with salt and pepper.

3. Grate the carrots and toss with the remaining 2 tablespoons of carrot juice and the vinaigrette. Season to taste with salt and pepper.

4. For an Elizabethan touch, arrange the grated carrots in a flower shape on the serving platter. Spoon the shrimp on the carrots to form the center of the flower. Sprinkle with the lemon zest. Serve with lemon wedges.

Another [Sallet for fish days]

Carret rootes being minced, and then made in the Dish, after the proportion of a flowerdeluce, then picke Shrimps and lay upon it with oyle and Vineger.

THE GOOD HUSWIFES JEWELL, 1587

In winter, carrot juice was added to butter to achieve the golden glow of butter churned in the summer when the cows ate richer grasses. Writing about carrots, the fifteenth-century cookbook author Platina notes, "There is nothing more pleasant to eat than this." Introduced into England by the Romans in the first century, carrots reached a height of popularity in the early 1600s as a Lenten food, for their resemblance to meat.

Renaissance Garden

*T*ALL ROSEMARY BRANCHES ornamented with fresh cherries anchored in lemons halves, as called for in the original recipe, were a typical Renaissance salad garnish. Other elaborate instructions in this recipe specified that the salad be served on a substantial platter suitable for a roast and that height be added by placing a roll under the greens. Boiled eggs studded with almonds and dates alternated around the platter with clusters of capers and candied orange and lemon slices. This attention to detail attests to the special status given salads in Shakespeare's day.

¼ cup verjuice

¼ cup grapeseed oil

2 teaspoons light brown sugar

Salt and freshly milled black pepper

6 cups assorted fresh herbs and baby lettuces

    (such as flat-leaf parsley, mint, endive,

    spinach, mesclun mix, or basil)

¼ cup capers, rinsed and drained

¼ cup golden raisins

½ cup blanched, slivered almonds

¼ cup currants

8 pitted dates, quartered lengthwise

6 dried figs, thinly sliced

4 long, sturdy fresh rosemary branches (optional)

2 large lemons, halved (optional)

12 fresh or candied whole cherries (optional)

2 large lemons, thinly sliced (optional)

¼ cup Candied Citrus Peel (page 237; optional)

1. Whisk together the verjuice, grapeseed oil, and brown sugar in a small bowl. Season to taste with salt and pepper.

2. Combine the herbs and lettuces, capers, raisins, almonds, currants, dates, and figs in a large bowl. Add the vinaigrette and toss until well coated.

3. If you are re-creating the original salad presentation, press 1 rosemary branch into the rounded end of each lemon half. Using the stem, a wire, or ribbon, attach 3 cherries to each rosemary branch.

4. Invert a small bowl or place a dinner roll in the center of a very large serving platter for additional height. Arrange the salad mix over and around the bowl. Place the rosemary branches at the 4 sides of the platter and arrange the lemon slices and citrus peel around the platter.

5. For an even more elaborate traditional Elizabethan garnish, alternate lemon slices topped with capers with quartered hard-boiled eggs, candied orange peel, and egg "porcupines" made by inserting almond and date slivers into hard-boiled-egg halves.

In Shakespeare's time olive oil was the most prized of all oils for salads. Grapeseed, walnut, and almond oils were also frequently used in salads and cooking. Rapeseed oil, now known as canola oil, was another kitchen staple.

You will not see balsamic vinegar mentioned in any of the Elizabethan salad recipes. Balsamic vinegar was only used medicinally back then.

Spring Lettuce with Chive Flowers

SERVES 6

And I think this word 'sallet' was born to do me good . . .

HENRY VI, PART II, 4.10

THIS LEMONY vinaigrette purée of chives with their springtime purple flowers perfectly complements delicate pre-summer baby lettuces and herbs.

The original recipe calls for the washed salad greens to be dried "in a strainer." Many of the simple kitchen appliances we take for granted today, such as salad spinners, had to be improvised in Shakespeare's day. A whisk was made with thin willow twigs tied together, and icing was brushed on with a rabbit's foot or bird's feather. A bale of hay hanging from the ceiling served as a knife holder, while quills were used to close the ends of stuffed fish or meats, much as we use toothpicks today.

2 tablespoons freshly squeezed lemon juice

2 tablespoons wine vinegar

¾ cup extra-virgin olive oil

3 tablespoons chopped fresh chives

Salt and freshly milled black pepper

1 cucumber, peeled and very thinly sliced

1 lemon, peeled and thinly sliced

½ cup assorted baby lettuces

1 cup assorted herb leaves (such as flat-leaf

parsley, hyssop, mint, sage, sorrel, or basil)

8 chive flowers

1. Purée the lemon juice, vinegar, olive oil, and chives until smooth. Season to taste with salt and pepper.

2. Toss the cucumber, lemon slices, lettuces, and herbs with the vinaigrette, place on a serving platter, and sprinkle with the chive flowers.

To make a sallet of all kinde of hearbes

Take your hearbes and picke them very fine into faire water, and pick your flowers by themselves, and wash them all cleane, and swing them in a Strainer, and when you put them into a dish, mingle them with cuwcumbers or lemmons, payred and sliced, and scrape sugar, and put in Vineger and oyle, and throw the flowers on the toppe of the sallet, of every sorte of the aforesaid thinges, garnish the dish about with the aforesaid things, and hard Egges, boyled, and laid about the dish and upon the sallet.

THE GOOD HUSWIFES JEWELL, 1587

Endive Topped with Periwinkles

SERVES 6

My salad days,
When I was green in judgement . . .

ANTONY AND CLEOPATRA, 1.5

SHAKESPEARE, LIKE MANY Englishmen of his day, knew quite a bit about plants, and throughout his works he makes numerous references to herbs, weeds, and flowers. Periwinkle, with its pretty five-petal purple-blue flower, looks like violets, and indeed it was often called "sorcerer's violet," as it was used in love charms and potions to drive away evil spirits.

The original recipe calls for "periwinkles," the snail-like mollusk. Taking poetic and culinary license, I chose to reinterpret this ingredient as the flower.

¾ cup extra-virgin olive oil

¼ cup honey vinegar (or any sweet vinegar)

3 tablespoons honey

Salt and freshly milled black pepper

3 heads of endive

½ cup periwinkles or other edible flowers

1. Whisk together the olive oil, vinegar, and honey in a small bowl and season to taste with salt and pepper.
2. Cut the endive into thin slices, removing the tough inner core, and toss with the vinaigrette.
3. Place some of the endive in the center of each plate and top with the flowers.

ORIGINAL RECIPE:

Another [Sallet for fish dayes]

White endiffe in a Dish with Periwinkles upon it, and Oyle and Vineger.

THE GOOD HUSWIFES JEWELL, 1587

Winter Salad with Raisin and Caper Vinaigrette

SERVES 6

For you there's rosemary and rue; these keep
Seeming and savour all the winter long . . .

THE WINTER'S TALE, 4.4

MOST OF THE salads in Shakespeare's time contained dried fruit such as figs, dates, raisins, and currants. These imports from Spain and Greece were considered elegant, healthful additions to salads. For variety, I puréed the dried fruit in the original recipe into the dressing. The result was fantastic and this is now my favorite dressing even on non-Shakespeare nights.

⅓ cup large raisins

¼ cup French apple cider vinegar

¾ cup extra-virgin olive oil

1 tablespoon light brown sugar

2 tablespoons small capers, rinsed and drained

Salt and freshly milled black pepper

½ cup mixed black and green olives

2 beets, boiled, peeled, and thinly sliced

2 lemons, peeled and sliced paper thin

1 long English cucumber, thinly sliced

1 cup shredded savoy cabbage

1. Place the raisins, vinegar, olive oil, brown sugar, and capers in a small food processor and purée until smooth. Place the vinaigrette in a small jar with a lid. Season to taste with salt and pepper and shake vigorously just prior to serving.

2. Place the olives in the center of a large serving platter. Layer the beets, lemon slices, cucumber, and cabbage around the olives. Drizzle the vinaigrette over the platter.

Watercress with Roasted Parsnips

SERVES 4

If music be the food of love, play on;
Give me excess of it . . .

TWELFTH NIGHT, 1.1

ᏢARSNIPS, BROUGHT TO England by the Ancient Romans, were much appreciated for their
natural sweetness and, like many sweet-tasting foods, were thought to "provoke lust."
Here parsnips pair well with the slightly bitter flavor of the watercress.

½ cup almond oil

3 tablespoons apple cider vinegar

¾ teaspoon salt

Dash of freshly milled black pepper

1 teaspoon light brown sugar

2 parsnips

2 bunches of watercress

2 tablespoons chopped mint leaves

2 tablespoons chopped flat-leaf parsley leaves

1. Whisk together the almond oil, vinegar, salt, pepper, and brown sugar in a small bowl.
2. Preheat the oven to 400°F. Peel the parsnips and slice ¼ inch thick. Place the slices on a lightly buttered baking sheet and roast for 15 to 20 minutes, or until tender. Toss the warm parsnips with half of the vinaigrette and arrange the slices around the edges of a serving platter.
3. Toss the watercress, mint, and parsley with the remaining vinaigrette and place in the center of the platter.

Mediterranean Orange and Caper Salad

SERVES 6

THIS SALAD RECIPE was specified for "great feasts" and the "prince's table." Interestingly, not all tables at a feast received the same foods. The more elaborate dishes and rare delicacies such as roast swan or porpoise were served only to the head table. Guests of lower rank probably never even saw this gorgeous salad.

½ cup almond oil

5 pitted green olives

1 tablespoon almond butter (available at health
   food stores, or use 1 tablespoon ground
   blanched almonds)

¼ cup freshly squeezed orange juice

1 tablespoon capers, rinsed and drained

2 tablespoons freshly squeezed lemon juice

Salt and freshly milled black pepper

2 cups baby spinach leaves

1 small head of red-leaf lettuce, cut into bite-size
   pieces

1 cucumber, thinly sliced

¼ cup assorted black and green olives, not pitted

5 fresh figs, sliced

Peeled lemon and orange slices

1. Place the almond oil, olives, almond butter, orange juice, capers, and lemon juice in a food processor and purée until smooth. Season to taste with salt and pepper.

2. Toss the spinach, lettuce, and cucumber with the vinaigrette and place in the center of a serving platter. Arrange the olives, figs, and lemon and orange slices around the plate.

Feasts offered not only special foods but entertainment also. Singers, jugglers, and dancers amused diners, or actors were hired to perform a play. For example, Shakespeare wrote *A Midsummer Night's Dream* to be performed at a wedding celebration and *Love's Labour's Lost* for a nobleman's private showing.

. . . Therefore let us devise
Some entertainment for them in their tents.
LOVE'S LABOUR'S LOST, 4.3

Sallet of Lemmons

SERVES 4

. . . She was the sweet-marjoram of the sallet, or rather,
the herb of grace.

ALL'S WELL THAT ENDS WELL, 4.5

THIS SALAD IS especially nice eaten with crusty bread and assorted olives, as was done in Shakespeare's day. It is excellent served with fish and also makes a lovely palate cleanser between courses.

In England, health writers and physicians recommended salad as a first-course appetite stimulant, while on the Continent medical authorities suggested it be eaten at the end of the meal to "close the stomach," a difference that still persists in Europe today.

2 lemons

1 tablespoon granulated white sugar

1 tablespoon colored crystal sugar

1. Using a sharp knife, peel the lemon zest in long strips and remove any white pith. Julienne the zest into $\frac{1}{8}$- by 1-inch strips. Bring 3 cups of water to a boil in a tea kettle or saucepan. Place the zest in a small saucepan and add 1 cup of boiling water. Boil the zest for 1 minute. Drain the water and run the zest under very cold water. Repeat this process two more times.

2. Cut the lemons into $\frac{1}{4}$-inch-thick slices, removing any seeds. Toss the lemons and zest with the granulated sugar and let stand for at least 1 hour.

3. Spoon the lemon salad in the center of each small plate and sprinkle the crystal sugar around the salad.

To Make a Sallet of Lemmons

Cut out slices of the peele of the lemmons long wayes, a quarter of an inch one peece from another, and then slice the lemmon very thinne and lay him in a dish crosse and the peeles about the lemons and scrape a good deale of Sugar upon them and so serve them.

THE GOOD HUSWIFES JEWELL, 1587

Grilled Tuna with Carrots and Sweet Onions

SERVES 4

How sweet the moonlight sleeps upon this bank!

THE MERCHANT OF VENICE, 5.1

*T*HE ROMANS WHO settled in Britain in the first century A.D. planted onions so they could prepare their favorite Mediterranean dishes. According to Boorde, an Elizabethan health writer, onion "maketh a man's apetyde good, and putteth away fastydyousness." Onions were thought to help one sleep soundly and even were prescribed to cure deafness and baldness.

The cool, crisp onion–carrot salad provides a refreshing crunch to the warm grilled tuna.

½ cup extra-virgin olive oil

3 tablespoons sherry vinegar

Salt and freshly milled black pepper

1 pound fresh tuna, cut into 8 long, thin slices

½ sweet onion (such as Vidalia), very thinly sliced

2 carrots, grated

4 lemon wedges

½ cup cooked whole grain such as wheat berries,

bulgur, or buckwheat (optional)

1. Whisk together the olive oil and vinegar and season with salt and pepper. Spoon 3 tablespoons of the vinaigrette onto the tuna, cover with plastic wrap, and refrigerate for 1 hour.
2. Preheat the grill. Season both sides of the tuna with salt and pepper. Grill the tuna for 1 to 2 minutes on each side, or until rare in the center.
3. Combine the onion and carrots in a small bowl and toss with the remaining vinaigrette.
4. Arrange the onion mixture in the shape of an oak leaf in the center of a platter. Top with tuna slices. Serve lemon wedges on a side plate. If using, scatter the grains over the salad.

Another [sallet for fish days]

Onyons in flakes layd round about the dish, with minced carrets layd in the middle of the dish, with boyled hoppes in five parts, like an oken leafe; made and garnished with tawney, long cut, with oyle and vineger.

THE GOOD HUSWIFES JEWELL, 1587

Watercress Salad with Sherry Pears

SERVES 4

*S*HERRY WAS A FREQUENT ingredient in Elizabethan cookbooks, and Shakespeare mentions both sherry and sack more than sixty times in his works. This English love of sack inspired me to poach the pears in sherry and purée them into a sherry vinaigrette.

1 cup sweet sherry

2 firm Comice or Bosc pears, peeled and sliced
½ inch thick

¼ cup sherry vinegar

¾ cup walnut oil

1 tablespoon sugar

Salt and freshly milled black pepper

2 bunches of watercress, stemmed

1. Bring the sherry to a simmer in a small saucepan over medium heat. Add the pears and cook for 20 minutes, or until just tender.

2. Purée half of the pear slices, the vinegar, walnut oil, and sugar until smooth and season to taste with salt and pepper.

3. Toss the watercress with the vinaigrette and arrange the reserved pears on and around the salad.

Vegetives

'Tis known, I ever

Have studied physic, through which secret art,

By turning o'er authorities, I have,

Together with my practice, made familiar

To me and to my aid the blest infusions

That dwell in vegetives, in metals, stones;

And I can speak of the disturbances

That nature works, and of her cures . . .

PERICLES, 3.2

. . . .

Vegetables, or "vegetives" as the Elizabethans called them, were served both raw and cooked with every meal. Herbs and various wild edible plants seasoned every dish. The "sweet herbs" so often called for in Elizabethan recipes were understood to mean an assortment of herbs and greens including lettuces and root tops. The Elizabethans used many more herbs than we do today, including those rarely seen in modern kitchens, such as hyssop, pennyroyal, tansy, and rue. According to a sixteenth-century nutrition guide, *A Dyetary of Healthe,* "There is no Herbe, nor weede, but God hae given vertue to them, to helpe man."

Puréed Carrots with Currants and Spices

S E R V E S 6

Let me see; what am I to buy for our sheep-shearing feast?
Three pound of sugar, five pound of currants . . .

THE WINTER'S TALE, 4.3

URRANT" IS AN anglicization of the Old French *raisin de Corinthe*, referring to the Greek city from which the dried fruit was imported to Britain. With their naturally high sugar content, currants appealed to the Elizabethan sweet tooth. In 1610 the Venetian ambassador to London wrote, "England ... consumes a greater amount of this fruit than all the rest of the world."

Carrots, here delicious paired with currants, were believed to be aphrodisiacs, "a great furtherer of Venus her pleasure, and of loves delights."

8 medium carrots, cut into 1-inch pieces

1 tablespoon verjuice

1 tablespoon butter

⅛ teaspoon ground cinnamon

2 tablespoons ginger marmalade

1 tablespoon currants

Salt and freshly milled black pepper

Bring 2 cups of salted water to a boil. Add the carrots, cover, and cook for 25 minutes, or until tender. Drain the carrots and purée with the verjuice, butter, and cinnamon until very smooth. (A tablespoon of the cooking liquid may be added if the mixture is too dry.) Stir in the marmalade and currants and season to taste with salt and pepper.

Poetry was very popular in Elizabethan England not only in plays and sonnets but also in cook-books. Thomas Tusser, a contemporary of Shakespeare's, wrote "Five Hundred Good Points of Husbandry" entirely in rhyme. About fruit Tusser wrote,

> Fruit gathered too timely will taste of the wood
> Will shrink and be bitter, and seldom prove good:
> So fruit that is shaken, and beat off a tree,
> With bruising and falling, soon faulty will be.

Sautéed Mushrooms "in the Italian Fashion"

SERVES 4

*M*USHROOMS, ALSO CALLED toadstools in England, were exceptionally popular in Renaissance Italy. You'll notice that this and many Elizabethan recipes call for cooking in either oil or clarified butter, butter precooked and strained. In keeping with the recipe's Italian origins, olive oil is used in this modern version. These mushrooms are delicious warm or cold, but if you are eating them cold add a bit more vinegar and oil just before serving.

> 2 tablespoons extra-virgin olive oil
> 8 cups sliced assorted mushrooms (such as
>   cremini, white button, or portobello)
> ¼ cup finely chopped mint
> ½ cup finely chopped flat-leaf parsley
> 1 tablespoon finely chopped thyme
> ½ cup finely chopped endive
> ⅛ teaspoon ground cinnamon
> 1 tablespoon verjuice
> Salt and freshly milled black pepper

Heat the olive oil in a large sauté pan. Add the mushrooms and cook for 1 minute. Add the mint, parsley, thyme, endive, and cinnamon, cover, and cook for 2 minutes. Stir in the verjuice and season to taste with salt and pepper.

ORIGINAL RECIPE:

To dress Mushrooms in the Italian Fashion

Take mushrooms, peel & wash them, and boil them in a skillet with water and salt, but first let the liquor boil with sweet herbs, parsley, and a crust of bread, being boil'd, drain them from the water, and fry them in sweet sallet oyl; being fried serve them in a dish with oyl, vinegar, pepper, and fryed parsley. Or fry them in clarified butter.

THE ACCOMPLISHT COOK, 1660

Crisp Fried Baby Artichokes

SERVES 4

Green indeed is the colour of lovers . . .

LOVE'S LABOUR'S LOST, 1.2

*I*N SHAKESPEARE'S TIME artichokes were thought to be an aphrodisiac. Only the bottoms were eaten and the leaves, if used at all, were only for garnish. The original sauce remains in this modern version, but whole baby artichokes substitute for the bottoms recommended in the original recipe.

8 baby artichokes

2 tablespoons freshly squeezed lemon juice

¼ cup extra-virgin olive oil

Salt and freshly milled black pepper

1 tablespoon verjuice

Zest of 1 orange

8 to 10 fresh mint leaves, finely chopped

1. Remove any tough outer leaves from the artichokes and cut off the thorny tops. Cut each artichoke in half and sprinkle with a little of the lemon juice to prevent darkening. Wrap each artichoke in a clean cloth. Using a meat mallet, or the flat part of a small frying pan, lightly pound the artichokes to flatten them slightly.

2. Heat the olive oil in a sauté pan over high heat for 1 to 2 minutes, or until it gets slightly smoky. Place the artichokes in the pan and cook for 3 to 4 minutes on each side, or until golden brown and the edges are crispy.

3. Arrange the artichokes in the center of a serving platter and season to taste with salt and pepper. Drizzle the verjuice on the artichokes and sprinkle with the orange zest and mint.

Beet and Apple Tarts

SERVES 6

I WAS INTRIGUED BY the title of this 1631 recipe, "A Fridayes Pye," not only because of the odd spellings of Friday and pie, but because it highlighted the fact that in Shakespeare's time neither fish nor meat was eaten on Fridays.

Served with assorted cheeses and a salad, these tarts make a wonderful nonmeat dinner.

½ recipe of Renaissance Dough (page 239)

2 tablespoons butter, melted

¼ teaspoon freshly milled black pepper

Dash of ground ginger

¼ cup raisins

¼ cup freshly squeezed orange juice

1 teaspoon sugar

2 medium beets, peeled and grated

1 Granny Smith apple, cored and finely diced

1. Preheat the oven to 400°F. Roll the Renaissance Dough to ⅛ inch thick on a floured work surface. Cut the dough into twelve 4-inch circles and press into muffins cups. (The dough will go about halfway up the sides of the muffin cup.) Bake for 4 minutes.

2. Lower the oven temperature to 350°F. Combine the butter, pepper, ginger, raisins, orange juice, and sugar in a bowl. Add the beets and apple and stir well. Spoon the mixture into the tart shells and bake for 20 minutes, or until the beets are tender. Allow to cool slightly in the pan before carefully removing.

A Fridayes Pye, without either Flesh or Fish

Wash greene Beets cleane, picke out the middle string, and chop them small with two or three well relisht ripe Apples. Season it with Pepper, Salt, and Ginger: then take a good handfull of Raisins of the Sunne, and put them all in a Coffin of fine Paste, with a peece of sweete Butter, and so bake it: but before you serve it in, cut it up, and wring in the juice of an Orange and Sugar.

MURRELLS TWO BOOKES OF COOKERIE AND CARVING, BOOK 1, 1615

"Coffin," as used in this recipe, meant a pie covered with a top crust. *Coffin* comes from the Middle French *cofin* for basket or holder. Pies and coffins were rectangular, square, or round and often had crusts thick enough to support the filling without an outer pan.

Why, thou say'st true; it is a paltry cap,
A custard-coffin, a bauble, a silken pie:
I love thee well, in that thou lik'est it not.
THE TAMING OF THE SHREW, 4.3

Six Onions Simmered with Raisins

*C*ULTIVATED SINCE prehistoric times, onions were a food staple for the common man in England. This onion dish is a wonderful accompaniment to meat, poultry, or fish and also makes a nice topping for toasted French bread as an appetizer or first course.

1 sweet Spanish onion, thinly sliced

1 small red onion, thinly sliced

1 small Vidalia onion, thinly sliced

2 leeks, thinly sliced (white part only)

3 scallions, diced

2 tablespoons extra-virgin olive oil

½ cup golden raisins

1 teaspoon five-color peppercorns, coarsely crushed

2 tablespoons dark brown sugar

1 teaspoon salt

¼ cup verjuice

1 tablespoon chopped chives

1. Sauté the onions, leeks, and scallions in the olive oil over medium-high heat for 15 minutes, or until just brown on the edges. Add the raisins, pepper, brown sugar, and salt and cook for 2 minutes, or until the onions are tender. Remove from the heat and stir in the verjuice.
2. Place the onion mixture in a serving bowl and sprinkle with the chives.

To Boil Onyons

Take a good many onyons & cut them in fowre quarters, set them on the fire in as much water as you thinke will boyle them tender, & when they be cleane skimmed, put in a good many smal raysins, halfe a spoonfull of grose Pepper, a good peece of Sugar, and a little Salt, and when the onyons be through boyled, beat the yolke of one egge with vergious and put into your pot, and so serve it upon soppes. If you will poch egges and laie upon them.

THE GOOD HUSWIFES JEWELL, 1587

Lemony Sweet Potatoes with Dates

SERVES 6

*D*ATES, A PREHISTORIC fruit of Arab origin, were imported into England in the thirteenth century. They were considered extremely healthful, especially for pregnant women, and were prized for their sweetness at a time when sugar was prohibitively expensive. In this recipe, dates are puréed to give a crunchy glaze to sweet potatoes flavored with lemon liqueur.

This recipe's tart and sweet mix nicely complements many of the recipes in the Fowle chapter, such as Stuffed Turkey Breast "French Fashion" (page 122).

2 large, long sweet potatoes, baked

½ cup lemon liqueur (such as limoncello)

¼ teaspoon ground mace

8 pitted dates, chopped

½ teaspoon salt

1 tablespoon butter

2 tablespoons light brown sugar

1. Peel the sweet potatoes and slice in circles.

2. Preheat the broiler. Purée the lemon liqueur, mace, dates, and salt until smooth. Place the purée in a saucepan and boil for 2 minutes. Place the sweet potatoes in a well-buttered baking dish and spread the purée over them. Dot the butter over the potatoes and sprinkle with the brown sugar. Broil for 1 to 2 minutes, or until the edges and topping are golden brown.

White potatoes, although introduced into England during Shakespeare's lifetime, were not commonly eaten until late in the eighteenth century. White potatoes originated from South America but were misnamed "Virginia potatoes" because they were thought to have come from the Virginia colony in America.

Another vegetable from the New World, corn, was also misnamed and called *granoturco*, "grain of Turkey," by Europeans. Jerusalem artichokes, truly one of the most misnamed of the New World foods, are not from Jerusalem and are not even in the artichoke family!

Other New World foods such as limes, grapefruits, tomatoes, and chile peppers were discovered by European explorers and introduced into Europe during Shakespeare's lifetime. However, these vegetables and fruits did not become available or even accepted as foods until a century after Shakespeare's death. Tomatoes were probably the last food to enter the European diet. Because tomatoes are in the nightshade family and their leaves are noxious to the taste, they were believed to be poisonous.

Spinach and Endive Sauté

SERVES 6

*L*EMONS WERE BROUGHT to England from Palestine during the Crusades led by English king Richard the Lionhearted. By the time of Shakespeare's birth, lemon trees were growing on many noblemen's estates. In the original recipe the herbs were fried with lemon slices to make a fritter. Here, raw lemons are added at the last minute to keep the greens bright but still provide the hint of tartness found in the Elizabethan version.

2 garlic cloves, minced

3 tablespoons extra-virgin olive oil

¼ cup red wine

6 ounces baby spinach

1 large head of endive, thinly sliced

1 bunch of flat-leaf parsley, stemmed and chopped

¼ teaspoon dried savory

Salt and freshly milled black pepper

2 lemons, thinly sliced

Zest of 1 lemon

Dash of freshly ground nutmeg

1. Cook the garlic in the olive oil on low heat for 1 minute. Add the wine, bring to a boil, and cook for 10 minutes, or until most of the wine has evaporated. Add the spinach, endive, parsley, and savory and cook, stirring constantly, for 1 minute, or until the greens are just wilted. Season to taste with salt and pepper.

2. Spoon the greens onto a serving platter and arrange the lemon slices around the platter. Sprinkle the lemon zest and nutmeg over the greens.

Cabbages with Smoked Duck

ℭABBAGE WAS THOUGHT to ward off drunkenness and prevent hangovers. Whether for that reason or simply because it was readily available, cabbage frequently appeared on feast menus. Oddly, recipes came with warnings that to eat reheated cabbage was fatal. "Twice cooked cabbage is death," an ancient adage popular in the Renaissance, referred both to that belief and to the tedium of listening to a comment repeated over and over.

I liked the Elizabethan notion of mixing cabbage and duck, but not wanting to cook an entire duck, I substituted prepared smoked duck breast that I purchased at my grocer. The smoky flavor added a perfect touch to the cabbage. Served with brown bread this makes a wonderful midweek dinner or weekend lunch. By the way, it reheats beautifully!

2 medium onions, diced

1 tablespoon butter

1 tablespoon extra-virgin olive oil

3 cups diced green cabbage

¼ cup Renaissance Stock (page 240)

1 cup slivered smoked duck meat

4 cups diced kale

1 cup diced savoy cabbage

Salt and freshly milled black pepper

Preheat the oven to 375°F. Sauté the onions in the butter and olive oil in an ovenproof baking dish over medium heat for 10 minutes, or until soft. Stir in the green cabbage, Renaissance Stock, and duck and bake for 30 minutes. Add the kale and bake for 15 minutes. Remove from the oven, stir in the savoy cabbage, and season to taste with salt and pepper.

To boyle a Mallard with cabbedge

Take some cabbedge and pricke & wash them cleane, and perboyle them in faire water, then put them into a collender, and let water run from them cleane, then put them into a faire earthen pot, and as much sweete broth as will cover the cabbadge, and sweete butter, then take your Mallard and rost it halfe enough, and save the dripping of him, then cut him in the side, and put the mallard into the cabbedge and put in all your drippings, then let it stew an houre, and season it with salt, and serve it upon soppes.

THE GOOD HUSWIFES JEWELL, 1587

Baby Cauliflower in Orange-Lemon Sauce

*I*N THE ORIGINAL recipe the chef specifies to cut off the cauliflower roots because the roots and leaves were usually cooked with the vegetable.

Taking a cue from the Elizabethans, on both not wasting and on cooking foods in broth, I now save leftover meat scraps and vegetables and tie them into a little sack made with cheesecloth closed with kitchen string. I add this sack to the cooking water for a sort of instant broth and flavor boost when I'm steaming vegetables or cooking pasta or rice.

6 heads of baby cauliflower

2 cups Renaissance Stock (page 240)

2 tablespoons butter

Zest of 1 lemon

2 tablespoons freshly squeezed lemon juice

Zest of 1 orange

$\frac{1}{2}$ cup freshly squeezed orange juice

Salt

1. Clean the cauliflower, leaving on some of the green leaves. Bring the Renaissance Stock to a boil in a pot with a steamer insert. Steam the cauliflower for 15 minutes, or until tender, and drain.

2. Combine the butter, lemon zest, lemon juice, orange zest, and orange juice in a large saucepan and simmer for 3 minutes. Season to taste with salt.

3. Place the cauliflower in a shallow serving bowl and pour the sauce over the cauliflower.

ORIGINAL RECIPE:

Buttered Colliflowers

Have a skillet of fair water, and when it boils put in the whole tops of the colliflowers, the root being cut away, put some salt to it; and being fine and tender boiled dish it whole in a dish, with carved sippets round about it, and serve it with beaten butter and water or juyce of orange and lemon.

THE ACCOMPLISHT COOK, 1660

Orange-Scented Rice

SERVES 4

> . . . Rice,—what will this sister of mine do with rice?
> But my father hath made her mistress of the feast, and she lays it on.
>
> *THE WINTER'S TALE, 4.3*

COSTLY PERFUME INGREDIENTS such as ambergris and musk, with little or no flavor of their own, were often called for in Elizabethan recipes to add fragrance. Here, cooking the rice in orange juice, orange zest, and crystallized ginger adds fragrance as well as a lovely flavor.

1¾ cups Renaissance Stock (page 240)

¼ cup orange-flavored liqueur (such as Cointreau)

1 teaspoon salt

1 cup white rice

¼ cup freshly squeezed orange juice

1 2-inch cinnamon stick

1 tablespoon butter

1 teaspoon sugar

2 tablespoons crystallized ginger

Zest of 1 orange

1. Bring the Renaissance Stock, orange liqueur, and salt to a boil. Add the rice, cover, and simmer over medium-low heat for 10 minutes. Add the orange juice, cinnamon stick, butter, sugar, and ginger, cover, and simmer for 15 minutes, or until the rice is tender.

2. Place the rice in a serving bowl and sprinkle with the orange zest.

To make a tart of Ryce

Boyle your ryce, and put in the yolkes of two or three Egges into the ryce and when it is boyled, put it into a dish, and season it with Sugar, Synamon and ginger and butter, and the juyce of two or three orenges, and set it on the fire againe.

THE GOOD HUSWIFES JEWELL, 1587

Dry rice from India was introduced into Italy in Roman times. It was planted in the Lombardy region of Italy during the Middle Ages and was exported on spice ships to England where, initially, it was a very expensive luxury.

Autumn Squashes with Apples and Fried Parsley

SERVES 6

And yet this time remov'd was summer's time,
The teeming autumn, big with rich increase,
Bearing the wanton burthen of the prime . . .

SONNET 97

THE FRIED PARSLEY adds a nice crunch and flavor to this wonderful fall dish. Parsley was eaten both raw and cooked in Shakespeare's day and was prescribed in remedies, including decoctions to counteract poisons and ease stomachaches. Queen Elizabeth I was known to have loved stewed parsley. According to *The Herball*, a botany book written in 1597, parsley "leaves are pleasant in sauces and broths . . . and agreeable to the stomach."

I especially like the taste boost apple cider vinegar gives to the squash.

1 teaspoon butter

1 cup plus 1 tablespoon extra-virgin olive oil

1 large yellow onion, thinly sliced

1 small butternut squash, thinly sliced lengthwise

1 small acorn squash, thinly sliced in rounds

1 red apple, sliced in rounds

Salt and freshly milled black pepper

2 tablespoons French apple cider vinegar

1 cup flat-leaf parsley leaves

1. Melt the butter in 1 tablespoon of the olive oil in a large sauté pan over low heat, add the onion, and cook for 2 minutes. Add the squashes and apple, cover, and cook for 5 to 6 minutes, or until the squash is tender. Season to taste with salt and pepper. Remove from the heat and sprinkle with the vinegar.

2. Heat the remaining 1 cup of olive oil to 350°F in a small saucepan. Place half of the parsley in the oil and fry for 10 seconds. Remove with a slotted spoon and drain on paper towels. Repeat the process with the remaining parsley and season with salt.

3. Place the squash, apple, and onion in a shallow serving bowl. Sprinkle the fried parsley around the sides of the bowl and serve immediately.

Other ways [to butter gourds]

Fry them [gourds] in slices, being cleans'd & peel'd, either floured or in batter; being fryed, serve them with beaten butter, and vinegar, or beaten butter and juyce of orange, or butter beaten with a little water, and served in a clean dish with fryed parsley, elliksanders [buds of the alexander flower], apples, slic't onions fryed, or sweet herbs.

THE ACCOMPLISHT COOK, 1660

Sweet Pea Purée with Capers

SERVES 4

*I*N THIS QUOTE Shakespeare is making a pun on "caper," which means both to leap and the pickled flower buds of the caper bush. As Shakespeare also notes, caper sauce was often eaten with mutton.

The combination of mint, peas, and capers in this recipe creates a light side dish, perfect for the spring and summer when fresh mint is plentiful. It is an especially nice accompaniment to lamb or fish.

1 pound peas (fresh or frozen)

½ cup coarsely chopped mint

3 tablespoons coarsely chopped flat-leaf parsley

2 tablespoons butter

¼ cup capers, rinsed and drained

Salt and freshly milled ground pepper

2 sprigs of mint

1. Place the peas in boiling water and cook for 5 minutes, or until done. Drain the peas and place in a food processor with the mint, parsley, and butter. Purée until smooth. Add the capers and pulse twice. Season to taste with salt and pepper.

2. Spoon the pea mixture into a serving bowl and top with the mint sprigs.

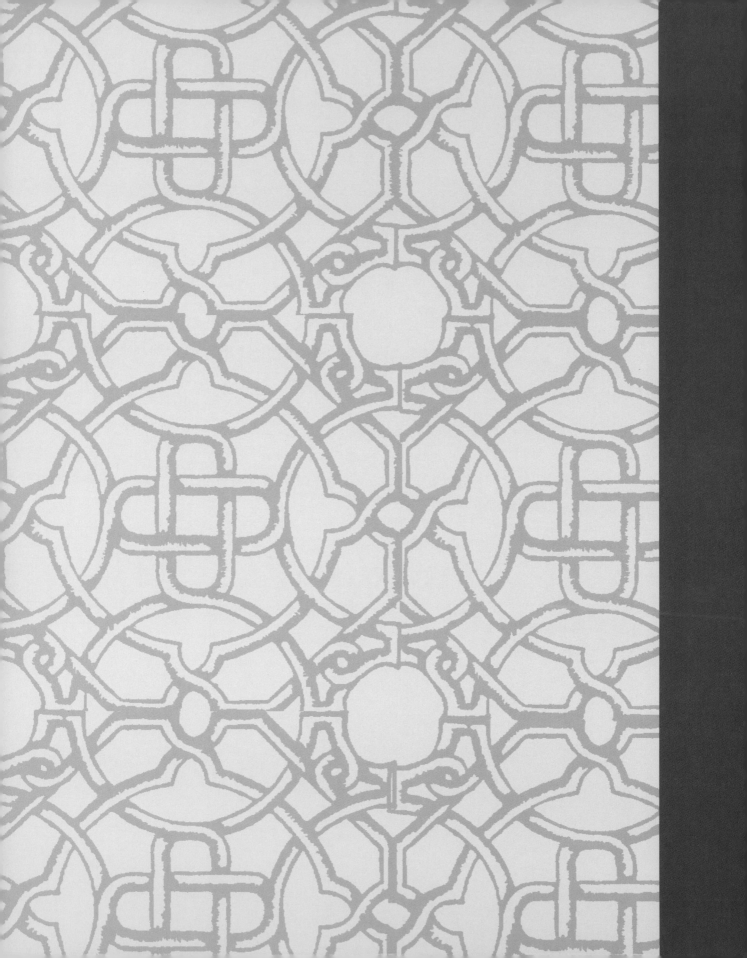

CHAPTER FIVE

ROASTED PHEASANT WITH CURRANTS AND WINE

CAPON WITH PEPPERCORN AND ONION STUFFING

CHICKEN WITH WINE, APPLES, AND DRIED FRUIT

CHICKEN AND ARTICHOKES

STUFFED TURKEY BREAST "FRENCH FASHION"

CORNISH GAME HENS WITH SAGE

CHICKEN PLUM PIE

DUCK BREAST WITH GOOSEBERRIES

ALMOND SAFFRON CHICKEN IN BREAD

CHICKEN WITH SORREL PESTO

fowle

Here on this grass-plot, in this very place,
To come and sport: her peacocks fly amain . . .

THE TEMPEST, 4.1

. . . .

Peacock, long a symbol of nobility and immortality, was one of the most esteemed feast foods in Shakespeare's time. Served roasted and placed back in its feathers, it was then dusted with real gold. Metal rods were inserted into the bird's body so that it remained upright and seemingly alive. The peacock would be made to appear to breathe fire by the cook's trick of placing a bit of camphor-soaked cotton in its mouth and lighting it just before serving. Despite these elaborate preparations, peacock was not considered tasty. Wrote one 1599 author, "Peacocke, is very hard meate, of bad temperature, and as evil juyce."

Roasted Pheasant with Currants and Wine

SERVES 4 TO 6

*I*N SHAKESPEARE'S DAY, the pheasant's drumsticks were tipped with gold leaf, and the prettiest feathers from the bird were added for a festive touch. For elegant dishes such as pheasant, the serving platter was often garnished with carved vegetables and fruit cut to look like flowers, baskets, or animals.

¼ cup currants

¼ cup white wine

4 ounces pancetta, diced

4 ounces ground pork

¼ teaspoon ground cloves

½ teaspoon ground mace

1 teaspoon salt

6 whole chestnuts, roasted and peeled

2 artichoke bottoms, cooked and diced

2 tablespoons pine nuts

2 tablespoons coarsely chopped pistachios

1 large egg, beaten

1 pheasant (3½ to 4 pounds)

Salt and freshly milled black pepper

1 tablespoon extra-virgin olive oil

1. Soak the currants in the wine for 1 hour.
2. Preheat the oven to 375°F. Cook the pancetta in a small sauté pan over medium heat for 1 minute, or until some fat is released. Add the pork, cloves, mace, and salt and cook for 5 minutes, or until the meat is done. Remove from the heat and stir in the chestnuts, artichoke bottoms, pine nuts, pistachios, and egg.
3. Season the outside and cavity of the pheasant with salt and pepper. Gently pack the stuffing in the cavity and under the neck flap. Brush the pheasant with the olive oil, place on a rack in a roasting pan, and roast for 1 hour, or until the leg juices run clear and the internal temperature is 160°F.
4. If you wish, decorative foil tips can be used to re-create the gilding that would have capped the drumsticks.

Other forcing for any dainty Foul; as Turkie,
Chickens, or as Pheasants, or the like boil'd or rost

Take minced veal raw, and bacon or beef-suet minc't with it; being finely minced, season
it with cloves and mace, a few currans salt, and some boiled bottoms of artichocks cut in
form of dice small, and mingle amongst the forcing, with pine-apple-seeds, pistaches,
chesnuts and some raw eggs, and fill our poultrey, & c.

THE ACCOMPLISHT COOK, 1660

Chefs strived to entertain guests with their culinary feats, creating such whimsical concoctions
as the mythical creature the "cockatryce," a combination of capon legs and the body of a suck-
ling pig. Robert May, the author of *The Accomplisht Cook,* amused diners by baking deer-shaped
baked dough filled with red wine so it appeared to "bleed" when pierced. He also built a table-
size battlefield with dough battleships and tiny dough cannons ignited by real gunpowder and
even provided the ladies with eggshells filled with scented water to be thrown on the floor to dis-
pel the scent of the gunpowder.

Ring, bells, aloud; burn, bonfires,
clear and bright,
To entertain great England's lawful king.
KING HENRY VI, PART II, 5.1

Capon with Peppercorn and Onion Stuffing

SERVES 6

Wherein is he good, but to taste sack and drink it? wherein
neat and cleanly, but to carve a capon and eat it?

KING HENRY IV, PART I, 2.4

*T*HIS ORIGINAL RECIPE was for a bread-based sauce for roast capon. Wood and cooking fuel were costly, so the working class often purchased already roasted meats from shops and street vendors. Cookbooks frequently contained recipes for sauces for these ready-made foods.

In this modern version, the sauce ingredients are used to create a spicy stuffing for the capon.

1 capon (about 6 pounds)

2 tablespoons freshly squeezed lemon juice

Salt and freshly milled black pepper

1 tablespoon butter, melted, plus 1 tablespoon
    cold butter

2 large Vidalia onions, small diced

2 tablespoons extra-virgin olive oil

1/2 cup plus 2 tablespoons red wine

3 cups cubed whole-wheat crusty country bread

Zest of 1 lemon

1/4 cup freshly squeezed orange juice

1/2 tablespoon five-color peppercorns, coarsely
    ground

1 cup Renaissance Stock (page 240)

1. Sprinkle the skin and cavity of the capon with the lemon juice and season with salt and pepper. Brush the skin with the melted butter.

2. Preheat the oven to 400°F. Sauté the onions in the olive oil over low heat for 20 minutes. Raise the heat to high and cook for 2 minutes, or until the onions are golden brown. Add 2 tablespoons of the wine and cook for 1 minute, or until the wine is absorbed. Remove from the heat and fold in the bread cubes, lemon zest, orange juice, and peppercorns. Season with salt and spoon the stuffing into the capon.

3. Place the capon on a lightly buttered roasting pan and bake for 1 hour to 1 hour and 20 minutes, depending on the weight of the capon, or until the leg juices run clear. Baste with the pan juices every 10 minutes for the final 30 minutes.

4. Deglaze the pan with the remaining ½ cup red wine. Cook on medium-high heat for 5 minutes, or until reduced to about 2 tablespoons. Strain through a fine-mesh sieve and return to the pan. Add the Renaissance Stock and cook for 5 minutes, or until reduced to about ½ cup. Remove from the heat and whisk in the cold butter.

5. Place the capon on a serving platter and serve the sauce in a small side dish.

ORIGINAL RECIPE:

Sauces for a roast Capon or Turkie

To make an excellent sauce for a roast Capon; you shall take Onions and having sliced and pilled them, boile them in faire water with pepper, salt, and a fewe bred crummes: then put unto it a spoonfull or two of Claret wine, the juice of an Orenge, and three or fowre slices of Lemmon pill; all these shred together, and so powre it upon the Capon being broke up.

THE ENGLISH HUSWIFE, 1587

Romans introduced the practice of gelding to England, changing chickens into tender, plump capons. In *The Castle of Health,* William Elyot wrote, "The capon is above all other fowles praised for as much as it is easily digested."

The carving term for a capon was to "sauce" it, a much prettier term than some of the others for cutting fowl, such as "disfigure that peacock," "spoil that hen," "dismember the heron," "unbrace the mallard," and "thigh that pigeon."

Chicken with Wine, Apples, and Dried Fruit

SERVES 4

> . . . Thou best of gold art worst of gold:
> Other, less fine in carat, is more precious,
> Preserving life in med'cine potable . . .
>
> *KING HENRY IV*, PART II, 4.5

*G*OLD WAS A commonly prescribed curative and thought to "[conserve] the youth and health." The original recipe is rather elaborate and was obviously intended for the rich, as "a peece of Golde" is placed between each section of chicken. The lid was then sealed shut with pastry to keep all the moisture and juices in the meat. This modern version omits the gold but keeps all the other rich flavors.

4 chicken legs and thighs

Salt and freshly milled black pepper

¼ cup whole-wheat flour

1 tablespoon extra-virgin olive oil

2 cups dry white wine

¼ cup currants

½ cup dried plums

½ cup pitted dates

1 tablespoon minced fresh ginger

½ teaspoon freshly ground nutmeg

½ teaspoon ground cinnamon

1 tart apple, cored and quartered, skin on

1. Cut apart the chicken legs and thighs. Sprinkle the chicken pieces with salt, pepper, and flour. Heat the olive oil in large sauté pan over high heat and brown the chicken on all sides. Remove the chicken from the pan. Add ¼ cup of the wine to the pan and stir to loosen the pan drippings. Add the remaining 1¾ cups of the wine, the currants, dried plums, dates, ginger, nutmeg, cinnamon, and apples. Return the chicken to the pan, cover with a tight lid, and reduce heat to low. Simmer, stirring occasionally, for 30 minutes, or until the chicken is very tender. Remove the chicken from the pan and cook the pan sauce for 5 to 10 minutes, or until reduced by half.

2. Place the chicken on a serving platter and pour the sauce over the chicken.

To stew a Cocke

You must cutte him in five pieces and washe him cleane and take Prunes, currants and dates, cutte very small and Raysins of the Sunne, and Sugar beaten very small, Cynamon, Ginger and nutmeggs likewise beaten, and a little Maydens [apples] cutte very small, and you must put him in a pipkin, and put in almost a pint of Muskadine, and then your spice and sugar uppon your Cocke, and put in your fruite betweene every quarter, and a peece of Golde betweene every peece of your Cocke, then you must make a lidde of Wood to fit for your pipkin, and close it as close as you can with paste, that no ayre come out, nor water can come in . . .

THE GOOD HUSWIFES JEWELL, 1587

Chicken and Artichokes

SERVES 6

> If sack and sugar be a fault, God help the wicked! if to be old and
> merry be a sin, then many an old host that I know is damned . . .
>
> *KING HENRY IV*, PART I, 2.4

ACK, A SWEET wine like sherry, was a favorite of Shakespeare. This delicious recipe "on the French fashion" slowly simmers chicken in wine, lemons, and a touch of sugar.

In *Dyets Drie Dinner*, a 1599 book on dining and health, the author makes a pun on the word *lemon* and "leman," the Elizabethan term for a lover. "All say a Limon in wine is good: some think a Leman and wine better."

3 tablespoons extra-virgin olive oil

1 chicken, cut into 8 pieces (about 4 pounds)

½ cup whole-wheat flour

¼ cup Renaissance Stock (page 240)

¾ cup white wine

1 lemon, unpeeled, diced, seeds removed

¼ teaspoon ground mace

6 dates, pitted and chopped

1 tablespoon brown sugar

1 teaspoon salt

5 to 6 artichoke bottoms, cleaned, parboiled

Heat the olive oil in a large sauté pan over medium-high heat. Dredge the chicken pieces in the flour and brown the chicken on all sides. Remove the chicken from the pan and add the Renaissance Stock, wine, lemon, mace, dates, brown sugar, and salt. Bring to a boil and add the chicken and artichokes. Reduce heat to medium, cover, and simmer for 30 minutes. Turn over the chicken and cook for 15 minutes, or until the chicken is fork tender.

Stuffed Turkey Breast "French Fashion"

SERVES 8

Contemplation makes a rare turkey-cock of him;
how he jets under his advanced plumes!

TWELFTH NIGHT, 2.5

TURKEYS WERE INTRODUCED to Europe from the Americas by Spanish explorers in the late 1500s. Thinking the bird, like so many other new and exotic delicacies, was from the country Turkey, it was consequently misnamed.

1 turkey breast, boned (about 3 pounds)

Salt and freshly milled black pepper

5 minced shallots

8 ounces prosciutto, minced

3 tablespoons butter, melted

2 tablespoons extra-virgin olive oil

750 milliliters white wine

1 quart Renaissance Stock (page 240)

3 bay leaves

3 sprigs of rosemary

6 whole cloves

2 mace blades

2 tablespoons whole black peppercorns

1. Starting from the meat side, cut a vertical slit into each half of the turkey breast, being careful not to cut through to the skin. Season both sides of the turkey breast with salt and pepper. Combine the shallots, prosciutto, and butter and spread one quarter of the mixture into each of the slits. Spread the remaining shallot mixture on the meat side of one of the breast halves and top with the other half of the turkey breast. Wrap the turkey in cheesecloth to keep the skin in place and the stuffing inside and tie securely with kitchen string.

2. Heat the olive oil in a large skillet and cook the turkey for 20 minutes, or until very brown on all sides.

3. Place the wine in a pot large enough to hold the turkey and bring to a boil. Add the Renaissance Stock, bay leaves, rosemary, cloves, mace, and peppercorns, reduce heat to very low, and add the turkey breast. Cover and simmer for 1 hour. Remove the turkey from the liquid and let cool. Refrigerate until ready to serve.

4. Slice the turkey and serve on a platter with bowls of assorted mustards.

Cornish Game Hens with Sage

SERVES 2

*I*N THE ORIGINAL recipe the cooked meat was minced, seasoned, and replaced back under the skin. In this simpler modern version the seasonings are tucked under the skin and into the hen's cavity before roasting for a lovely hint of sage throughout. The English gave sage its name because they believed that if taken regularly the herb would promote wisdom.

Although chickens were much smaller in Shakespeare's day, Cornish game hens did not exist in his lifetime. These tasty birds were developed in America in the late 1800s.

½ cup butter, softened, plus 1 teaspoon butter

1 tablespoon plus ¼ teaspoon finely chopped sage
     leaves, plus 6 more leaves and more to
     garnish

2 tablespoons minced shallot

½ teaspoon ground mace

1 tablespoon finely chopped flat-leaf parsley

1 teaspoon salt

2 Cornish game hens

2 shallots, sliced

¼ cup plus 2 tablespoons wine

½ cup Renaissance Stock (page 240)

Pinch of freshly grated nutmeg

¼ cup cream

Salt and freshly milled black pepper

Fresh red currants, for garnish (optional)

1. Preheat the oven to 375°F. Combine the ½ cup of softened butter, 1 tablespoon of the chopped sage leaves, 1 tablespoon of the minced shallot, the mace, parsley, and salt. Spread the mixture under the skin and in the cavity of the hens. Place 3 sage leaves, 1 sliced shallot, and 2 tablespoons of the wine in the cavity of each hen and bake for 40 minutes, or until the leg juices run clear.

2. Melt the remaining 1 teaspoon of butter in a saucepan, add the remaining 1 tablespoon of minced shallot, and cook for 2 minutes. Add the remaining ¼ cup of wine and boil for 2 minutes. Add the

Renaissance Stock, the remaining ¼ teaspoon of chopped sage, and the nutmeg and bring to a simmer. Reduce to low heat, add the cream, and season to taste with salt and pepper.

3. Place the Cornish hens on a serving platter. Arrange the currants and sage leaves around the hens, if desired. Serve the sauce in a small dish alongside the hens.

In the charming 1599 dietary, *Dyets Drie Dinner,* the author shares an Elizabethan fable on how pepper became black. According to the tale, pepper grew in a serpent-infested forest in a far-off land. The natives were terrorized by the serpents and finally decided to burn down the forest to drive away the dreaded creatures. Everything for miles around became charred and that is why to this day pepper is black.

Chicken Plum Pie

SERVES 6

> Shall I compare thee to a summer's day?
> Thou art more lovely and more temperate:
> Rough winds do shake the darling buds of May,
> And summer's lease hath all too short a date . . .
>
> SONNET 18

*T*HIS IS A LOVELY summer picnic dish that makes perfect use of leftover chicken. The nobility enjoyed outdoor dining in Shakespeare's day. A 1575 painting shows Queen Elizabeth I at a picnic during a hunt. One foreign visitor observed that when Queen Elizabeth dined, her ladies in waiting "gave to each of the Guards a mouthful to eat . . . for Fear of any Poison."

½ recipe of Renaissance Dough (page 239)

1 pound cooked chicken meat, shredded

3 tablespoons Renaissance Stock (page 240)

Pinch of ground cloves

½ teaspoon ground mace (or nutmeg)

¼ teaspoon ground cinnamon

4 purple plums, pitted, peeled, and diced

Salt and freshly milled black pepper

2 plums, cut in ¼-inch slices

2 tablespoons butter, melted

1 tablespoon light brown sugar

1. Preheat the oven to 375°F. Roll out the Renaissance Dough to ⅛ inch thick on a floured work surface. Press into a round or square pie pan and bake for 10 minutes, or until the bottom is very light golden.

2. Combine the chicken, Renaissance Stock, cloves, mace, cinnamon, and diced plums in a large bowl and season to taste with salt and pepper. Spoon the mixture into the piecrust and place the plum slices on top of the chicken mixture. Drizzle the butter over the top and sprinkle with the brown sugar. Bake for 40 minutes, or until the crust is golden and the plums are caramelized. (If serving the pie cold, double the quantity of mace, cinnamon, and cloves.)

To bake Chickens with Damsons

Take your Chickens, drawe them and wash them, then breake their bones, and lay them in a platter, then take foure handfuls of fine flower, and lay it on a faire boord, put thereto twelve yolks of Egs, a dish of butter, and a litle Saffron: mingle them altogether, & make you paste therewith. Then make six coffins, and put in every coffin a lumpe of butter of the bignesse of a Walnut: then season your six coffins with one spoonful of Cloves and Mace, two spoonfuls of Synamon, and one of Sugar, and a spoonfull of salt. Then put your Chickens into your pies: then take Damisons and pare away the outward peele of them, and put twentie in every of your pie, round about your chicken, then put into everie of your coffins a hand full of Corrans. Then close them up, and put them into the Oven, then let them be there three quarters of an houre.

THE GOOD HUSWIVES HANDMAIDE FOR THE KITCHIN, 1594

Duck Breast with Gooseberries

SERVES 4

*T*HE ELIZABETHANS ATE all sorts of fowl, including quail, crane, heron, buzzards, and pigeons. Partridge, like many of the other birds, was thought to "comforte the brayne and the stomachke, & . . . augment carnall lust."

Duck, both wild and domestic, was a favorite. In the original recipe the duck was boiled with gooseberries and served with the skin pale. This modern version retains all the interesting tart flavors of the original but produces a nice brown, crisp skin.

1 duck breast (about 1 pound)

1 large onion, sliced

½ cup white wine

2 endive leaves

3 sprigs of flat-leaf parsley

2 bay leaves

2 sprigs of thyme

1 cup Renaissance Stock (page 240)

6 ounces gooseberries (or tart fresh Morello
    cherries)

1. Score the duck breast with 3 diagonal slashes. Cook the duck, skin side down, in a skillet over very low heat for 15 to 17 minutes, or until the skin is dark brown and crispy. Drain the fat from the pan periodically as the duck cooks. Remove the duck from the pan.

2. Cook the onion slices in 1 tablespoon of the duck fat for 3 minutes. Add the wine, stirring to loosen the pan drippings, and cook for 3 minutes, or until the wine is almost evaporated. Tie together the endive, parsley, bay leaves, and thyme with kitchen string. Add the Renaissance Stock and the tied herbs to the pan. Place the duck in the pan, skin side up, cover, and cook over very low heat for 15 minutes. Remove the duck from the pan.

3. Strain the cooking liquid through a fine-mesh sieve and return to the pan. Add the gooseberries and mash them slightly with a fork. Cook for 4 minutes, or until the gooseberries are warm and soft.

4. Cut the duck breast into thin slices and arrange the slices in the center of each plate. Pour the gooseberry sauce over the duck.

The Latin phrase *Deliculo surgere saluberrium,* "to rise early is best," was well known to Shakespeare's Elizabethan audience. Renaissance dietaries cautioned against oversleeping in the morning, as the body might run out of the last meal's nutrients. Conversely, a nap after meals was encouraged to concentrate the body's energy on digestion.

Not only was the best time of day to eat outlined, but also what foods to eat at the different times of year. Elizabethan physicians advised eating according to the season, to balance the weather's effect on digestion. In warm weather, "cool and moist" foods such as fruits and vegetables and light meats like chicken were recommended. In the winter, "hot and dry" spices such as ginger, mustard, and pepper and "hot" meats such as mutton and beef were encouraged.

. . . Not to be abed after midnight is to
be up betimes; and 'diluculo surgere,'
thou know'st, —
TWELFTH NIGHT, 2.3

Almond Saffron Chicken in Bread

SERVES 6

*T*HIS TASTY DISH makes it seem as if you spent hours in the kitchen because it fills the air with the wonderful aroma of baked bread. In reality this English version of a French Renaissance classic is quick to assemble using day-old bakery-bought bread and leftover chicken seasoned with almonds, pistachios, herbs, and spices.

The French *pain mollet*, meaning soft bread, was misspelled as "pine-molet" in the original recipe.

4 saffron threads

4 ounces almond oil

1 large egg yolk

¼ teaspoon Dijon mustard

2 tablespoons almond paste

Salt and freshly milled black pepper

8 ounces cooked capon meat, shredded

12 almonds, chopped with skins on

2 cups finely chopped assorted fresh herbs and
    greens (such as sorrel, endive, flat-leaf
    parsley, baby spinach, or mint)

⅛ teaspoon dried marjoram

⅛ teaspoon dried sage

Pinch of cinnamon

⅛ teaspoon freshly ground nutmeg

¼ cup currants

2 tablespoons ground pistachios

1 round loaf of day-old French sourdough country
    bread (about 10 inches in diameter)

1 tablespoon butter, softened

1. Soak the saffron threads in the almond oil for 30 minutes.
2. Combine the egg yolk and mustard in a large bowl and slowly whisk in the almond oil until a mayonnaise forms. Whisk in the almond paste, season with salt, and combine with capon and almonds.

3. Place the fresh herbs and greens, marjoram, sage, cinnamon, nutmeg, currants, and pistachios in a bowl and mix well.

4. Preheat the oven to 375°F. Quickly put the bread under running water to dampen it. Cut a 4-inch circle in the top of the bread, remove the top circle of crust, and scoop out the soft bread inside the loaf. Spread the herb mixture in an even layer in the bottom and up the sides of the bread, reserving about ½ cup for the top. Spoon the capon mixture over the herbs, completely filling the cavity. Spread the reserved herbs over the capon and replace the top crust of the bread. Spread the butter on the bottom of the bread and wrap it tightly in aluminum foil. Bake for 50 minutes.

ORIGINAL RECIPE:

Another French boil'd meat of Pine-molet

Take a manchet of French bread of a day old, chip it and cut a round hole in the top, save the peice whole, and take out the crumb, then make a composition of a boild or a rost Capon, minced and stampt with Almond past, muskefied bisket bread, yolks of hard Eggs, and some sweet Herbs chopped fine, some yolks of raw Eggs and Saffron, Cinamon, Nutmeg, Currans, Sugar, Salt, Marrow and Pistaches; fill the Loaf, and stop the hole with the piece, and boil it in a clean cloth in a pipkin, or bake it in an oven . . .

THE ACCOMPLISHT COOK, 1660

"Bake it in an oven," as called for in the original recipe, meant cooking in an enclosed hot-air container, a method used as early as the Anglo-Saxon period, beginning in the fifth century A.D. Hot-air cooking, as we do in ovens today, was created in one of three ways: by lighting hot burning wood in an oven and then removing the ashes before placing the food in the oven; by placing food in an inverted pot and lighting a fire on or near the pot; or by building an oven into a structure so that hot air could be conducted around the oven in flues.

Chicken with Sorrel Pesto

SERVES 4

*T*HIS RECIPE calls for sorrel, thought to be an essential aid to digestion. According to the Elizabethan botany book *The Herbal*, sorrel is "a profitable sauce in many meats, and pleasant to the taste."

Food was deeply linked to medicine and well-being in Shakespeare's day. Most cookbooks contained recipes for the sick such as this one "for him that hath a weake stomacke." Physician Andrewe Boorde wrote, "God may sende a man good meate, but the deuyll may sende an evyll coke to dystrue it." He maintained that every cook is half physician and that good health is achieved through diet.

½ cup plus 1 tablespoon fresh sorrel leaves,
    chopped
¼ cup fresh flat-leaf parsley leaves
½ teaspoon dried savory
½ teaspoon dried thyme
1 garlic clove
2 tablespoons butter, softened
1 teaspoon brown sugar
2 tablespoons Renaissance Stock (page 240)
Salt and freshly milled black pepper
4 chicken breasts, pounded ¾ inch thick

1. Purée ½ cup of the sorrel, the parsley, savory, thyme, and garlic in a small food processor. Add the butter, brown sugar, and Renaissance Stock and blend until creamy. Season to taste with salt and pepper.

2. Preheat the grill. Season the chicken breasts with salt and pepper. Brush the breasts with 2 tablespoons of the pesto. Grill for 1 to 2 minutes on each side, or until the juices run clear.

3. Place a chicken breast in the center of each plate and top with a dollop of pesto. Sprinkle the remaining 1 tablespoon of sorrel around the plate.

CHAPTER SIX

LAMB CHOPS WITH ALE AND DRIED FRUIT

ROAST LEG OF LAMB WITH MINT—CAPER SAUCE

RACK OF LAMB "IN THE FRENCH FASHION"

LEG OF LAMB WITH OYSTER STUFFING

ROAST VENISON MARINATED IN WINTER HERBS

HERBED VEAL ROLLS

RENAISSANCE "APPLE" AND STEAK PIE

STEAK WITH ELDERBERRY MUSTARD

PRIME RIB ROAST WITH ORANGE-GLAZED ONIONS

SIMMERED BEEF "HODGEPODGE" WITH SHERRY—PARSLEY SAUCE

ROASTED PORK WITH HERBS AND GRAPES

Meate

I spy entertainment in her; she discourses, she carves,

she gives the leer of invitation . . .

THE MERRY WIVES OF WINDSOR, 1.3

. . . .

It was considered an honor to be asked to carve at a feast, and knowing how to properly slice meats was a sign of good breeding. Elizabethan cookbooks included not only carving instructions, but the proper terminology for each type of meat such as "breake that deer, leach that brawn, lift that swan, unbrace that Mallard, allay that Fesant, wing that partridge, disfigure that peacock, dismember hern, and unlace that coney."

Lamb Chops with Ale and Dried Fruit

SERVES 6

*D*ATES WERE OFTEN paired with meat in the sixteenth and seventeenth centuries, as they were thought to provide balance to meat's heaviness and "heat." An Elizabethan physician notes in *The Haven of Health* that dates "are commonly used at delicate feasts, to set forth other meats, and are counted restorative."

Dates certainly do add a delicious flavor and texture to this wonderful lamb dish.

2 large onions, thinly sliced

3 sprigs of rosemary

4 sprigs of thyme

1/4 cup chopped flat-leaf parsley

1/2 teaspoon ground cinnamon

1/2 teaspoon ground ginger

1/2 teaspoon freshly ground nutmeg

4 whole cloves

12 loin lamb chops

1 teaspoon salt

1/2 teaspoon freshly milled black pepper

8 large dried plums, halved

4 dried apricots

1/4 cup raisins

10 dates, halved and pitted

1/4 cup currants

12 ounces ale or beer

1. Preheat the oven to 375°F. Lay the onion slices on the bottom of a lightly buttered baking pan. Scatter the rosemary, thyme, parsley, cinnamon, ginger, nutmeg, and cloves over the onions. Season the lamb chops with the salt and pepper and lay in a single layer over the herbs. Sprinkle the plums, apricots,

raisins, dates, and currants over the chops and pour on the ale. Cover tightly with aluminum foil and bake for 30 minutes, or until the meat is cooked to medium.

2. Preheat the broiler. Remove the aluminum foil from the pan and broil the lamb chops for 2 to 3 minutes, or until the meat is browned.

3. Spoon the onions and dried fruits in the center of a serving platter and top with the lamb chops. Drizzle the cooking juices over the chops.

ORIGINAL RECIPE:

To make stewed steaks

Take a peece of Mutton and cut it in peeces, and wash it verie cleane, and put it into a faire pot with Ale, or with half wine, then make it boyle, and skumme it cleane, and put into your pot a faggot of rosemarie and time: then take some parsely picked fine, and some onions cut round, and let them all boyle together, then take prunes, & reasons, dates and currants, and let it boyle altogether, and season it with Sinamon and ginger, Nutmegs, two or three Cloves, and Salt, and so serve it on soppes, and garnish it with fruite.

THE GOOD HUSWIFES JEWELL, 1587

Since the Middle Ages, pieces of toasted bread have been added to beer and wine to improve the beverages' flavor. It is from that practice that we get the expression "to drink a toast." In Shakespeare's day there was also another saying, "not worth a toast," meaning not worth a crust of bread.

Go fetch me a quart of sacke,
put a toast in 't.
THE MERRY WIVES OF WINDSOR, 3.5

Roast Leg of Lamb with Mint-Caper Sauce

SERVES 10 TO 12

I tell thee, Kate, 'twas burnt and dried away;
And I expressly am forbid to touch it,
For it engenders choler, planteth anger;
And better 'twere that both of us did fast,
Since, of ourselves, ourselves are choleric,
Than feed it with such over-roasted flesh.

THE TAMING OF THE SHREW, 4.1

THE ELIZABETHANS SUBSCRIBED to the ancient Greeks' belief that all substances are composed of the elements fire, air, water, and earth. "Does not our life consist of four elements?" asks Sir Toby Belch in *Twelfth Night*. Everything and even everyone was believed to possess some degree of cold, hot, moist, or dry qualities. Someone like Shakespeare's fiery-tempered Katharina the Shrew would have been considered "hot" and labeled "choleric."

To balance personality, Elizabethans thought that one ought to eat foods that possess qualities opposite to one's own disposition. Petruchio warns Kate not to eat meat, thought "hot," as it would only exacerbate her already excitable nature.

½ cup chopped endive

½ cup finely chopped flat-leaf parsley

½ cup plus 2 tablespoons finely chopped mint

½ cup finely chopped assorted greens (such as
      sage, watercress, or baby spinach)

½ cup dried bread crumbs

1½ tablespoons caraway seeds

1½ tablespoons coriander seeds

¼ cup diced Candied Citrus Peel (page 237)

⅛ teaspoon freshly grated nutmeg

6 dates, finely chopped

½ cup plus 2 tablespoons small capers, rinsed
      and drained

1 large egg

1 teaspoon brown sugar

continued

2 tablespoons verjuice

¼ cup minced marrow (or butter)

Salt and freshly milled black pepper

1 leg of lamb, boned and butterflied
     (5 to 6 pounds)

½ cup Renaissance Stock (page 240)

½ cup freshly squeezed orange juice

1 teaspoon granulated sugar

Zest of 1 orange

1. Preheat the oven to 350°F. Combine the endive, parsley, ½ cup of the mint, the greens, bread crumbs, 1 tablespoon of the caraway seeds, 1 tablespoon of the coriander seeds, the citrus peel, nutmeg, dates, ½ cup of the capers, the egg, brown sugar, verjuice, and marrow in a large bowl and season with salt and pepper. Season both sides of the lamb with salt and pepper. Spoon the mixture into the center of the lamb and tie closed with kitchen string. Place in a baking pan and bake for 1¼ hours, or until the internal temperature reaches 160°F for medium. Remove the lamb from the pan and let rest for 10 minutes. Meanwhile, bring the stock to a boil in a small sauce pan, until reduced by half.

2. Add the orange juice to the baking pan and stir well to loosen the pan drippings. Purée the pan drippings with the Renaissance Stock, the remaining 2 tablespoons of mint, the remaining 2 tablespoons of capers, and the granulated sugar until smooth. Stir in the orange zest and warm in a small saucepan.

3. Place the leg of lamb in the center of a serving platter and spoon the sauce over the lamb. Sprinkle the remaining ½ tablespoon of caraway and coriander seeds over the lamb and around the platter.

A Legge of Lambe searst with Hearbes

Strue it as before shewed, with sweet Hearbes and grated Bread, Bisket seeds, a few Coriander-seeds, Lemmon pills minst fine, Nutmeg sliced, sliced Dates, a little grosse pepper, Capers washt cleane: put all together with six or seven yolkes of new layd Egges, hard roasted and whole, & put them in your stuffe and worke them with Sugar, Rosewater and verjuyce, and the Marrow of a bone or two, Salt and pepper, put all together into the Skin: Carrawayes and Orangado are fittest garnish for your Dish.

MURRELLS TWO BOOKES OF COOKERIE AND CARVING, BOOK 1, 1615

Rack of Lamb "in the French Fashion"

SERVES 4

*T*HIS FRENCH-INFLUENCED dish calls for "lemon cut in square peeces like dice," which makes a beautiful and flavorful addition to the sauce. Since I began researching and preparing dishes from sixteenth- and seventeenth-century cookbooks, I have come to appreciate the extra flavor available from lemons and oranges diced whole and added to stews and sauces or puréed into salad dressings. Citrus fruits were rare and costly back then so no part, not even the skin, was wasted.

2 lemons

½ cup Renaissance Stock (page 240)

½ cup sweet sherry

½ teaspoon ground mace

¼ cup currants

½ teaspoon salt

¼ cup small capers, rinsed and drained

1 lamb rack (8 ribs)

1. Zest one of the lemons and place the zest in a small nonreactive saucepan. Zest the remaining lemon and chop the zest fine. Set the zest aside. Dice both of the peeled lemons (discarding the seeds), and add to the pan. Add the Renaissance Stock, sherry, mace, currants, salt, and capers to the pan and bring to a boil. Reduce the heat and simmer for 5 minutes. Remove from the heat and cool to room temperature.

2. Place the lamb in a nonreactive pan, pour the marinade over the lamb, and refrigerate for at least 3 hours or up to 24 hours.

3. Preheat the oven to 400°F. Remove the lamb from the marinade and place in a roasting pan. Roast in the center of the oven for 1 hour, or until the internal temperature reaches 160°F for medium. Remove the lamb from the oven and let rest for 10 minutes before carving.

4. Place the marinade in a small saucepan and bring to a simmer for 5 minutes, or until thick.

5. Place 2 ribs of lamb on each plate and spoon some of the marinade over the lamb. Sprinkle the reserved chopped lemon zest around the plate.

Leg of Lamb with Oyster Stuffing

SERVES 8

*O*YSTERS WERE OFTEN paired with meats, especially lamb, in Elizabethan cooking. Many oyster dishes, including our traditional American Christmas goose with oyster stuffing and Southern steak and oysters, have come to us by way of the first English settlers here. In this version, the oysters combine with a perfect mix of herbs and currants to create a subtle stuffing that even non-oyster lovers will enjoy.

¼ cup butter, melted

6 scallions

Zest of 1 lemon

½ cup finely chopped spinach

1 head of endive, finely chopped

½ cup finely chopped flat-leaf parsley

2 cups dried whole-wheat bread crumbs

2 large egg yolks

12 oysters, chopped, ¼ cup of the liquid reserved

¾ cup currants

2 teaspoons light brown sugar

1 teaspoon ground cinnamon

2 tablespoons verjuice

Salt and freshly milled black pepper

1 leg of lamb, boned and butterflied

½ cup white wine

1 tablespoon freshly squeezed lemon juice

1 tablespoon finely chopped mint

1. Preheat the oven to 350°F. Combine the butter, scallions, lemon zest, spinach, endive, ¼ cup of the parsley, the bread crumbs, egg yolks, oysters, ½ cup of the currants, the brown sugar, cinnamon, verjuice, and salt and pepper to taste. Spoon the mixture into the center of the lamb. Tie the leg of lamb closed with kitchen string and season with salt and pepper. Bake, basting occasionally with the pan juices, for 1 hour, or until the internal temperature reaches 160°F for medium. Remove the lamb from the pan and let rest for 15 minutes.

2. Place the cooking pan on the stovetop over medium heat, add the wine, and scrape all the solids from the bottom of the pan. Add the reserved oyster liquid, the remaining ¼ cup of parsley, the remaining ¼ cup of currants, the lemon juice, and the mint and cook for 3 to 5 minutes, or until warm.

3. Place the leg of lamb in the center of a serving platter. Drizzle a few tablespoons of the sauce over the lamb and serve the remaining sauce in a side dish.

Roast Venison Marinated in Winter Herbs

SERVES 8

> . . . Other women cloy
> The appetites they feed; but she makes hungry
> Where she most satisfies . . .
>
> *ANTONY AND CLEOPATRA, 2.2*

THERE ARE MANY poetic references to food in Shakespeare's *Antony and Cleopatra*. From correspondences between the real Marc Antony and his wife, we know that while visiting Cleopatra in Egypt he dined on "five or six courses" and ate venison.

In England, deer hunting was only permitted on lands owned by the hunter and, in fact, illegal hunting in royal forests was punishable by heavy fines and even death. Once you taste this easy-to-prepare roast you will know why venison was considered "a lordes dysshe . . . a meat for greate men."

1 cup red wine

3 tablespoons light brown sugar

1 tablespoon fennel seeds

1 tablespoon dried savory

1 tablespoon dried rosemary

1 tablespoon dried thyme

3 whole bay leaves

Venison loin (about 4 pounds)

½ teaspoon ground cinnamon

½ teaspoon freshly ground nutmeg

¼ teaspoon ground ginger

½ teaspoon salt

1 teaspoon freshly milled black pepper

½ cup butter

¼ cup verjuice

1. Heat the wine in a small saucepan. Add the brown sugar, fennel, savory, rosemary, thyme, and bay leaves and simmer for 5 minutes. Remove the pan from the heat and cool to room temperature. Place

the venison in a bowl and pour on the marinade. Cover tightly with plastic wrap and refrigerate for 8 hours, or overnight, turning the roast occasionally to ensure even marinating.

2.   Preheat the oven to 400°F. Remove the venison from the marinade, reserving the marinade. Place the roast in a baking pan and sprinkle the cinnamon, nutmeg, ginger, salt, and pepper over the roast. Dot with ¼ cup of the butter. Roast in the oven for about 45 minutes, or until the internal temperature reaches 145°F for medium. Allow the loin to rest for 10 to 15 minutes before carving.

3.   Meanwhile, simmer the reserved marinade for 40 minutes, stirring frequently. Strain through a fine-mesh sieve and whisk in the verjuice and remaining ¼ cup of butter. Serve the sauce in a small dish alongside the venison.

Herbed Veal Rolls

SERVES 6

> Wilt thou be gone? it is not yet near day:
> It was the nightingale, and not the lark,
> That pierc'd the fearful hollow of thine ear;
> Nightly she sings on yond pomegranate-tree . . .
>
> *ROMEO AND JULIET, 3.5*

STUFFED AND ROASTED larks were a rare delicacy in Shakespeare's time, so veal slices were often substituted for these tiny birds. In the original recipe the suggested list of herbs is extensive and includes all sorts of greens such as strawberry leaves and endive. Mixing an assortment of herbs, lettuces, and fruit leaves makes this veal filling delicious and unusual. Whenever possible, I now add crunchy endive and snips of organic, pesticide-free fresh fruit leaves to any recipe calling for fresh herbs.

½ cup currants

⅓ cup white wine

2 hard-cooked egg yolks

2 tablespoons butter, melted

6 dried plums, slivered

1½ cups chopped assorted lettuces and herbs
    (such as endive, spinach, chicory, parsley,
    thyme, sorrel, or strawberry leaves)

3 scallions, thinly sliced

12 very thin veal slices (approximately 3 by
    4 inches each)

Salt and freshly milled black pepper

2 tablespoons extra-virgin olive oil

¼ teaspoon ground mace

⅛ teaspoon ground cinnamon

⅛ teaspoon ground cloves

½ cup finely diced endive

¼ cup finely chopped flat-leaf parsley

12 long fresh chives (optional)

1. Soak the currants in the wine for 30 minutes. Drain, reserving the wine.

2. Mash the egg yolks and butter in a large bowl. Add the dried plums, currants, and 2 tablespoons of the wine from the currants and mix well. Toss in the lettuces and scallions and mix well. Season each slice of the veal with salt and pepper. Spread about 2 tablespoons of the lettuce mixture onto each veal slice, roll closed, and tie with kitchen string.

3. Place the olive oil in a large skillet and sear the veal for $1\frac{1}{2}$ to 2 minutes per side, or until browned. Add the remaining wine from the currants, the mace, cinnamon, and cloves and gently simmer for 2 to 3 minutes, or until the wine has evaporated.

4. Place 2 veal rolls in the center of each plate and sprinkle with the diced endive and parsley. If you like, snip the kitchen string and retie the rolls after cooking with long fresh chives.

Renaissance "Apple" and Steak Pie

SERVES 12

Look to the bak'd meats, good Angelica:
Spare not for cost.

ROMEO AND JULIET, 4.4

*S*LICES OF RICHLY seasoned steak are topped with tiny lamb meatballs that look like little apples because of the way the sprig of sage leaf is centered. This pie has no top crust, so guests can easily serve themselves to a succulent meatball and slice of steak.

Twelve ¼-inch-thick slices top round or boneless
  shell steaks (about 4 by 5 inches each)
1 teaspoon coarsely milled fresh pepper
1 teaspoon freshly ground nutmeg
½ teaspoon salt
1 pound ground lamb
½ teaspoon finely chopped flat-leaf parsley
½ teaspoon finely chopped thyme
½ teaspoon finely chopped sage
1 large egg
¼ cup cream
¼ cup raisins
½ recipe of Renaissance Dough (page 239)
¼ cup orange-flavored liqueur (or orange juice)
2 tablespoons verjuice
1 tablespoon butter
12 sage leaves

1. Pound the slices of steak with a meat hammer until very thin. Sprinkle the slices with the pepper, nutmeg, and salt, cover with plastic wrap, and refrigerate for at least 1 hour.
2. Combine the lamb, parsley, thyme, chopped sage, egg, cream, and raisins and form into 12 balls.
3. Preheat the oven to 350°F. Roll out the Renaissance Dough to ⅛ inch thick on a floured work surface.

Press the dough into a 9 by 13-inch baking pan, trimming any excess dough. Bake for 10 minutes, or until light golden brown.

4. Preheat the broiler. Broil the steaks and meatballs for 1 minute on each side. Line the bottom of the piecrust with the cooked steaks and top with the meatballs.

5. Place the orange liqueur in a small saucepan and simmer for 3 to 4 minutes. Whisk in the verjuice and butter and pour over the steak and meatballs. Poke a hole in the top of each meatball with a toothpick and insert a sage leaf to form the "apples."

ORIGINAL RECIPE:

To bake Steak Pies the French way

Season the steaks with pepper, nutmeg, and salt lightly, and set them by; then take a piece of the leanest of a leg of mutton, and mince it small with some beef suet and a few sweet herbs, as tops of tyme, penniroyal, young red sage, grated bread, yolks of eggs, sweet cream, raisins of the sun & c. work all together and make it into little balls, and rouls, put them into a deep round pye on the steaks, then put to them some butter, and sprinkle it with verjuyce, close it up and bake it, being baked cut it up, then roul sage leaves in butter, fry them, and stick them in the balls, serve the pye without a cover, and liquor it with the juyce of two or three oranges or lemons.

THE ACCOMPLISHT COOK, 1660

Steak with Elderberry Mustard

SERVES 4

THE MUSTARD for this grilled steak is made with elderberry wine and elderberry vinegar, but any berry liqueur and vinegar work well. For parties I set out the mustard ingredients and ask friends to mix their own. This way guests can adjust the ratio of hot to sweet to suit their taste.

London broil (about 1½ pounds)

½ teaspoon coarsely milled black pepper

⅛ teaspoon ground ginger

1 teaspoon coarsely ground coriander seeds

½ cup plus 2 tablespoons elderberry wine

¼ cup honey

1 tablespoon dry mustard

1 tablespoon elderberry vinegar

Salt and freshly milled black pepper

2 tablespoons butter, melted

1. Place the beef in a nonreactive pan and sprinkle with the pepper, ginger, and coriander. Pour ½ cup of the wine over the meat, cover with plastic wrap, and refrigerate for 8 hours, or overnight.

2. Combine the remaining 2 tablespoons wine, the honey, dry mustard, and vinegar in a small bowl. Season to taste with salt and pepper and set the mustard aside.

3. Preheat the grill. Remove the beef from the marinade, brush with 1 tablespoon of the melted butter, and grill for 5 minutes. Brush the uncooked side with the remaining 1 tablespoon of butter, turn over, and grill for 5 to 6 minutes, or until the meat is cooked to medium. Let rest for 5 to 10 minutes before cutting.

4. Serve with elderberry mustard on the side.

To Carbonado, broil or toast Beef in the Italian fashion

Take the ribs, cut them into steaks & hack them, then season them with pepper, salt, and coriander-seed, being first sprinkled with rose-vinegar, or elder vinegar, then lay them one upon another in a dish the space of an hour, and broil or toast them before the fire, and serve them with the gravy that came from them, or juyce of orange and the gravy boild together.

THE ACCOMPLISHT COOK, 1660

Carbonado was a method of cutting and notching meat for more even cooking. The term was derived from *carbone*, the Italian for charcoal. One 1615 recipe for beef carbonado came with a warning: "indeed a dish used most for wantonness!"

. . . He scotched him and notched him
like a carbonado.
CORIOLANUS, 4.5

Prime Rib Roast with Orange-Glazed Onions

SERVES 6

*T*O ROAST a Fillet of Beef," as indicated in the original recipe, meant skewering and turning it on a spit before an open fire.

In this modern version the onions are divided into two batches to create a nice combination of tender onions for the glaze and firm ones for a side vegetable.

6 large onions, quartered

1 cup finely chopped assorted fresh herbs (parsley,
    marjoram, tarragon, rosemary, or hyssop)

1 prime rib roast, bone in (about 10 pounds,
    6 ribs)

Salt and freshly milled black pepper

2 tablespoons verjuice

$\frac{1}{4}$ cup Renaissance Stock (page 240)

$\frac{1}{2}$ cup freshly squeezed orange juice

Zest of 1 orange

1. Preheat the oven to 350°F. Toss the onions and herbs in a roasting pan. Reserve half of the onions in a plastic bag. Season the prime rib with lots of salt and pepper and place on top of the herb–onion mixture. Roast for $1\frac{1}{2}$ hours, then add the remaining onions. Continue to roast for another hour, or until the internal temperature reaches 160°F for medium. Meanwhile, bring the stock to a boil in a small sauce pan until reduced by half.

2. Remove the meat from the pan and let rest. Add the verjuice and Renaissance Stock to the pan and stir to loosen the onions and drippings. Purée $\frac{1}{4}$ cup of the onions, the juices from the pan, and the orange juice until smooth and stir in the orange zest.

3. Place onions in the center of a serving platter and top with the roast. Serve the sauce in a side dish.

Simmered Beef "Hodgepodge" with Sherry-Parsley Sauce

SERVES 8

*O*PEN-FIRE ROASTING was a smoky affair that required almost constant turning and supervision. The more common method of cooking was to boil, as in this "hodge" or medley of ingredients. This parsley bread sauce is still made in many parts of Europe to serve with *bollito*, boiled or cold meats.

3 tablespoons extra-virgin olive oil

1 beef rump roast (3½ to 4 pounds)

3 bay leaves

1 large yellow onion, sliced

2 garlic cloves, crushed

1 carrot, cut into chunks

2 celery stalks, cut into chunks

1 large Vidalia onion, sliced

3 garlic cloves, coarsely chopped

1 tablespoon sugar

½ teaspoon coarsely milled black pepper

¾ cup finely chopped flat-leaf parsley

½ cup edible flowers

6 slices dense whole-wheat or seedless rye bread,
    crusts removed, torn into small pieces

¼ cup verjuice (or 2 tablespoons sherry vinegar)

2 tablespoons sherry

Salt

1. Place 2 tablespoons of the olive oil in a heavy-bottomed pot and brown the beef on all sides. Add the bay leaves, yellow onion, crushed garlic, carrot, celery, and enough water to cover three quarters of the beef. Bring to a simmer and cook for 1 hour.

2. Remove 2 cups of the cooking liquid from the pot and set aside for the sauce. Cover the pot and let rest.

3. Simmer the reserved cooking liquid for 30 to 45 minutes, or until reduced to about 1 cup.

4. Sauté the Vidalia onion in the remaining 1 tablespoon olive oil over low heat for 10 minutes, or until soft. Add ½ cup of the reduced stock, the chopped garlic, sugar, and pepper and simmer for 4 minutes. Cool slightly and purée with the parsley until smooth. Add the marigolds, bread, verjuice, and sherry and stir until combined. Season to taste with salt. If the sauce is too thick, add more of the reduced stock until it reaches a creamy consistency.

5. Serve the sauce in a dish alongside the beef.

ORIGINAL RECIPE:

To make a Hodgepodge

Boyle the neck of mutton or a fat rump of Beef, and when it is well boyled take the best of the broth and put it into a Pipkin, and put a good many Onions to it, two handful of marigold flowers, and a handful of Percely fine picked, and groce shred and not to small, and so boyle them in the broth: and thick it with strained Bread: putting therein groce beaten pepper, and a spooneful of Vinagre: and let it boyle some what thick, and so lay it upon your meat.

A BOOK OF COOKRYE, 1587

Roasted meats were served with a variety of condiments, the recipes for which were often borrowed from other countries. The Englishman Dr. Henry Buttes wrote in *Dyets Dry Dinner,* "The Italians, as all the world knows, is most exquisite in the composition of all sorts of Condiments." "Green sauce," one of many Italian-influenced condiments, was made of a sweet herb such as mint or basil crushed in a mortar with garlic, rose vinegar, cloves, and tart orange juice.

Roasted Pork with Herbs and Grapes

SERVES 8 TO 10

The capon burns, the pig falls from the spit,
The clock hath strucken twelve upon the bell;
My mistress made it one upon my cheek:
She is so hot because the meat is cold . . .

THE COMEDY OF ERRORS, 1.2

THE CRISP, slightly salty pancetta adds perfect contrast to the grape-and-herb stuffing. This is one of my favorite recipes because it is simple to prepare yet impressive to serve. As suggested in the original recipe, for a variation, substitute gooseberries for the grapes.

Dash of freshly ground nutmeg

1 tablespoon salt

1 teaspoon freshly milled black pepper

1 cup finely chopped flat-leaf parsley

2 endive stalks, finely chopped

½ cup assorted finely chopped herbs (such as
        thyme, mint, rosemary, savory, or sage)

½ cup currants

½ cup red seedless grapes, quartered

½ cup green seedless grapes, quartered

1 pork loin, butterflied (about 4 pounds deboned)

12 thin slices pancetta (about 4 ounces)

15 whole cloves

4 rosemary sprigs, cut into 16 pieces

Preheat the oven to 450°F. Combine the nutmeg, salt, pepper, parsley, endive, herbs, currants, and red and green grapes in a bowl. Spread the mixture in the center of the pork loin and tie with kitchen string. Place the pancetta slices over the pork loin and press in the cloves and rosemary tips to secure it. Roast for 15 minutes, reduce the oven temperature to 350°F, opening the oven door for a few minutes to reduce the heat quickly, and cook for 1 hour, or until the pork reaches an internal temperature of 140°F.

Otherways [to bake a pig]

Take a pig being scalded, flayed, and quartered, season it with beaten nutmeg, pepper, salt, cloves, and mace, lay it in your pie with some chopped sweet herbs, hard eggs, currans (or none) put your herbs between every lay, with some gooseberries, grapes or barberries, and lay on the top slices of interlarded bacon and butter, close it up, and bake it in good fine crust, being baked, liquor it with butter, verjuyce, and sugar. If to be eaten cold, with butter only.

THE ACCOMPLISHT COOK, 1660

CHAPTER SEVEN

SALMON IN PASTRY

SALMON ROLLS "PRICKED WITH A FEATHER"

CRAB WITH CAPERS AND GARLIC

GRILLED BASS WITH FENNEL

RED SNAPPER WITH CAVIAR

SAUTÉED TROUT WITH WINE AND HERBS

FLOUNDER WITH DRIED PLUMS

LOBSTER WITH PISTACHIO STUFFING AND SEVILLE ORANGE BUTTER

LOBSTER TAILS WITH WILDFLOWERS

SCALLOPS IN BERRY GLAZE

COD STEAKS WITH ONIONS AND CURRANTS

MUSSELS IN PASTRY

Fysshe

My gentle Puck, come hither. Thou rememb'rest

Since once I sat upon a promontory,

And heard a mermaid on a dolphin's back

Uttering such dulcet and harmonious breath

That the rude sea grew civil at her song

And certain stars shot madly from their spheres,

To hear the sea-maid's music.

A MIDSUMMER NIGHT'S DREAM, 2.1

. . . .

A great variety of all sorts of sea creatures were eaten in Shakespeare's day, including porpoise, dolphin, otter, and seal. There was even a recipe entitled Mermaid's Pie, a combination of eel, pork, and spices.

"Of all nacyons and countres, England is beste servd of Fysshe, not onely of al maner of see-fysshe, but also of fresshe-water fysshe, and of all maner of sortes of salt-fysshe," wrote Dr. Andrewe Boorde of his seafaring nation.

Salmon in Pastry

SERVES 12

Bait the hook well; this fish will bite.

MUCH ADO ABOUT NOTHING, 2.3

ISH PIES WERE often made into the shape of the fish being eaten, such as lobster, crab, salmon, or carp, and the crust was embellished with elaborate pastry scales, fins, gills, and other details. This recipe comes from the beautifully illustrated cookbook by Robert May that includes several foldout pages of various designs for pies, including ones decorated with multicolored sugars to resemble stained-glass windows.

If you prefer a quicker version, wrap the ingredients in parchment or aluminum foil instead of the pastry dough.

1 recipe of Renaissance Dough (page 239)

3 artichoke bottoms, cooked and quartered

1 salmon fillet, cut into twelve 2 by 3-inch pieces

(about 1½ pounds)

1 teaspoon salt

½ teaspoon coarsely milled black pepper

½ teaspoon freshly ground nutmeg

1 dozen medium oysters

12 thin asparagus spears, cut into 1-inch pieces

24 green seedless grapes or gooseberries

¼ cup coarsely chopped pistachio nuts

1 large egg, beaten

3 lemons, cut into wedges

1. Roll out slightly less than half of the Renaissance Dough into a 5 by 13-inch rectangle about ¼ inch thick and place on a parchment-lined baking sheet.

2. Place the artichokes in a long line down the center of the crust. Sprinkle the salmon with the salt, pepper, and nutmeg and place over the artichokes. Arrange the oysters, asparagus, grapes, and pistachios over the salmon.

3. Roll out the remaining dough into a 5 by 13-inch rectangle and place on top of the ingredients. Trim the dough into the shape of a fish and pinch the edges to seal. Using the excess dough, add fish details, such as an eye or fin. Using a teaspoon, imprint scale and tail marks on the dough, being careful not to cut through the dough. Brush with the egg and refrigerate for at least 30 minutes.
4. Preheat the oven to 375°F. Bake the salmon for 40 minutes, or until golden brown.
5. Serve with lemon wedges.

This recipe includes artichokes and asparagus, both considered aphrodisiacs in Elizabethan England. Artichokes originated in Sicily and were introduced into England by the Dutch. King Henry VIII's fondness for artichokes was legendary and he had them grown in his castle gardens. Artichokes, asparagus, and salmon were all expensive delicacies in Shakespeare's day enjoyed only by the wealthy nobility.

Salmon Rolls "Pricked with a Feather"

SERVES 4

*T*HE CHARMING ORIGINAL instructions suggest that the salmon slices be cut to "three fingers breadth" and "the length of a woman's hand." They were then rolled with a mouthwatering filling and "pricked with a feather, full closed." I have to confess that I tried the quills as suggested in the original 1596 directions and they caught fire!

½ cup currants

2 ounces finely ground salmon

½ cup lemon liqueur (such as limoncello)

¼ teaspoon ground mace

Dash of ground cloves

¼ teaspoon salt

¼ teaspoon freshly milled black pepper

Four 3 by 5-inch salmon slices, ¼ inch thick

1 tablespoon extra-virgin olive oil

1. Soak the currants and ground salmon in the lemon liqueur for 1 hour.

2. Preheat the broiler. Add the mace, cloves, salt, and pepper to the currant mixture and spread over the salmon slices. Roll up the slices and close with toothpicks that have been soaked in water. Brush the olive oil on the rolls and broil for 2 to 3 minutes per side, or until just golden at the edges.

Elizabethan tables were set with only a spoon and knife, and often even the knife was omitted, as guests frequently brought their own. Forks, fashionable in Italy, did not come into use in England or most other European countries until many years after Shakespeare's death.

An English travel writer, Thomas Coryat, first saw a fork in 1611 in Italy. Coryat speculated that "the Italian cannot by any means indure to have his dish touched with fingers." Coryat so admired this new invention that he ate with it throughout his travels and back home in England, where a dear friend nicknamed him "furcifer."

Salt was an important seasoning in Elizabethan times because of its ability to both enhance flavor and preserve food. As the word *salacious* suggests, salt was thought to stimulate the appetite and libido.

In the Middle Ages, part of a man's pay could be given in salt, leading to the expression "worth his salt." *Salary,* from the Latin *salarium,* literally means salt money.

Salt was expensive in the Middle Ages, so placing a salt dispenser near a guest was a sign of respect from the host. The lower a guest's rank the farther he was seated from the salt, giving rise to the expression "below the salt," meaning inferior.

Is not birth, beauty, good shape, discourse,
manhood, learning, gentleness, virtue, youth,
liberality, and such like, the spice and salt
that season a man?
TROILUS AND CRESSIDA, 1.2

Crab with Capers and Garlic

SERVES 4

Why, then, can one desire too much of a good thing?

AS YOU LIKE IT, 4.1

THE SUBTLE ADVICE in the original recipe to "rub the shells with a clove or two of garlick" prompted me to try what is surely one of the best Elizabethan crab dishes.

Crab was a popular and inexpensive food in England at that time and was even prescribed medicinally; for example, the shells were "burnt to ashes" as a remedy for "the biting of mad-dogs."

8 ounces crabmeat

¼ cup white wine

1 tablespoon port wine vinegar

⅛ teaspoon dried thyme

3 tablespoons fresh bread crumbs

1 large egg white, beaten well

1 rounded tablespoon capers, rinsed and drained

⅛ teaspoon ground mace

Salt and freshly milled black pepper

1 garlic clove, finely minced

1 tablespoon extra-virgin olive oil

1. Combine the crabmeat, wine, vinegar, thyme, bread crumbs, egg white, capers, and mace in a small bowl and season with salt and pepper.

2. Preheat the oven to 425°F. Cook the garlic and olive oil over low heat for 1 minute, or until warm. Brush the oil mixture into 4 tart molds or cleaned crab shells and fill with the crab mixture. Place on a baking sheet and bake for 15 minutes. Turn on the broiler and broil the crab for 2 to 3 minutes, or until the top is light golden brown.

To stew Crabs otherways

Being boil'd take the meat out of the shells, and put it in a pipkin with some claret wine, and wine vinegar, minced tyme, pepper, grated bread, salt, the yolks of two or three hard eggs strained or minced very small, some sweet butter, capers, and some large mace; stew it finely, rub the shells with a clove or two of garlick, and dish them as is shown before.

THE ACCOMPLISHT COOK, 1660

Grilled Bass with Fennel

SERVES 4

*S*HAKESPEARE WAS CLEARLY familiar with the classic Renaissance pairing of fish and fennel, as he refers to it in *King Henry IV*. The ancient Romans introduced fennel into England. It was eaten raw in salads or cooked in pottages, meat, and fish dishes. It was so popular that Gerard, a sixteenth-century botanist, didn't even include a detailed description of it in his botany book. "It is so well known amongst us, that it were but lost labour to describe the same."

1 tablespoon extra-virgin olive oil

1 cup thinly sliced fennel

$\frac{1}{4}$ cup plus 1 tablespoon finely chopped flat-leaf
parsley

$\frac{1}{4}$ teaspoon fennel seeds

Salt and freshly milled black pepper

2 bass fillets, halved (about 8 ounces each)

4 lemon wedges

1. Heat the olive oil in a small sauté pan and add the fennel. Cover and cook for 4 to 5 minutes, or until the fennel is softened. Add $\frac{1}{4}$ cup of the parsley and the fennel seeds and season to taste with salt and pepper. Cover and keep warm while the bass is cooking.

2. Preheat the grill or broiler. Season the bass with salt and pepper and cook for 2 to 3 minutes on each side, or until firm.

3. Place a bass fillet in the center of each plate and top with some of the fennel mixture. Sprinkle with the remaining 1 tablespoon parsley and place a lemon wedge on each plate.

Red Snapper with Caviar

SERVES 4

> . . . The play, I remember, pleased not the million;
> 'twas caviare to the general . . .
>
> *HAMLET, 2.2*

CAVIAR WAS A rare and exotic delicacy in the 1500s, and as Shakespeare points out in *Hamlet*, the general public did not appreciate it. The original recipe calls for "rones" or roe, but I have substituted caviar, which is available year-round. The tantalizing "sweet sawce" can be served in a hollow lemon half for a festive touch.

4 small red snapper or trout, head on (12 to
    14 ounces each)
¼ cup extra-virgin olive oil
Salt and freshly milled black pepper
12 dates, minced
¼ cup finely grated fresh ginger
8 ounces caviar
8 ounces fresh red currants or barberries (do not
    substitute dried currants)
1 tablespoon sugar
2 tablespoons freshly squeezed lemon juice

1. Preheat the broiler or grill. Brush the snapper inside and out with the olive oil and season with salt and pepper. Combine the dates and ginger and gently fold in the caviar. Spoon the mixture into the cavity of the snapper. Broil or grill the fish for 4 to 5 minutes on each side, or until the flesh is firm and opaque.

2. Place the currants, sugar, and lemon juice in a small saucepan and simmer for 10 minutes, or until slightly thickened. Purée until smooth.

3. Place a snapper in the center of each plate and serve the sauce in a small dish or hollow lemon half.

To rost a Carpe or Tench with a pudding in his bellie

Take the Rones of a Pike and choppe them verie small, then put in grated bread, two or three Egs, Currants, Dates, Suger, Sinemome and Ginger, and Mace, Pepper and salt, and put it in his bellie, and put him on a Broche, and make Sweet sawce with Barberies, or Lemmons minced, and put into the Sweete sawce and then put it on the Carpe when you serve him up.

THE GOOD HUSWIFES JEWELL, 1587

Sautéed Trout with Wine and Herbs

SERVES 4

. . . Here comes the trout that must be caught with tickling.

TWELFTH NIGHT, 2.5

A POPULAR EXPRESSION IN Shakespeare's day, "as found as a trout," meaning to be caught red-handed, came from the fact that trout are so easily caught.

The original recipe advised the reader to substitute water mixed with vinegar and sugar if wine was not available, a clue to the quality of the wine in England during Shakespeare's lifetime! Most English wine was imported from southern Europe in porous wooden casks that absorbed odors and impurities during the long ocean voyage.

4 trout, cleaned and boned

Salt and freshly milled black pepper

$\frac{1}{2}$ cup flour

$\frac{1}{2}$ cup plus 1 tablespoon finely chopped flat-leaf

    parsley

$\frac{1}{4}$ teaspoon dried savory

$\frac{1}{4}$ teaspoon dried thyme

4 small sprigs of rosemary

2 garlic cloves, crushed

$\frac{1}{4}$ cup extra-virgin olive oil

1 cup white wine

8 lemon wedges

1. Sprinkle the trout inside and out with salt and pepper and dredge in the flour. Combine $\frac{1}{2}$ cup of the parsley, the savory, and thyme in a small bowl. Place 1 to 2 tablespoons of the herbs and 1 rosemary sprig inside each trout.

2. Cook the garlic in the olive oil in a large sauté pan over low heat for 1 minute. Remove the garlic and turn the heat to medium-high. Add the trout, and cook for 2 minutes on each side, or until browned and crispy. Pour $\frac{1}{2}$ cup of the wine over the trout and cook for 2 minutes, or until the wine evaporates. Carefully turn over the trout, add the remaining $\frac{1}{2}$ cup of wine, and cook for 2 to 3 minutes, or until the wine evaporates.

3. Place the trout on a serving platter and sprinkle with the remaining 1 tablespoon of parsley. Season to taste with salt and pepper and arrange the lemon wedges around the platter.

Flounder with Dried Plums

SERVES 4

There's rosemary, that's for remembrance; pray, love, remember:
and there is pansies, that's for thoughts.

HAMLET, 4.5

A HANDFULL OF ROSEMARIE" is called for in the original recipe. Rosemary was a favorite herb of the time, a symbol of remembrance at funerals and weddings. Cookbooks even advised putting the leaves under the mattress to prevent "evil dreams," washing with it to keep your "face fair and the breath sweet," and placing it with woolen clothing and furs to keep them fresh.

1 cup white wine

2 tablespoons light brown sugar

$\frac{1}{2}$ teaspoon dried rosemary

$\frac{1}{2}$ teaspoon dried thyme

$\frac{1}{4}$ teaspoon dried marjoram

$\frac{1}{4}$ teaspoon dried savory

2 large whole mace (or $\frac{1}{8}$ teaspoon ground mace)

2 tablespoons currants

8 dried plums, thinly sliced

4 flounder fillets (about 6 ounces each)

Salt and freshly milled black pepper

1 tablespoon cold butter, cut into small pieces

1 tablespoon verjuice

1. Place the wine, brown sugar, rosemary, thyme, marjoram, savory, mace, currants, and plums in a sauté pan. Simmer, mashing the plums occasionally with a fork, for 3 to 4 minutes, or until some of the wine evaporates and the plums begin to dissolve.

2. Season the flounder with salt and pepper, place on top of the sauce, and cook for 2 minutes. Remove the pan from the heat, cover, and let stand for 1 to 2 minutes more, or until the fish is firm and opaque. Remove the flounder from the pan and keep warm.

3. Cook the pan sauce over high heat for 3 minutes, or until thickened. Add the butter and verjuice and whisk until emulsified.

4. Place a flounder fillet in the center of each plate and spoon the sauce over the fish.

Lobster with Pistachio Stuffing and Seville Orange Butter

SERVES 4

*L*OBSTER MEAT WAS served delicately cut and placed on bread "sippets" or minced and put back into the shell. The original recipe calls for the raw lobster meat to be taken out of the shell, which is not an easy thing to do. In this version the lobster is kept whole and the remaining "hash" ingredients are added as a pistachio stuffing with a tart Seville orange butter sauce.

4 lobsters (about 1½ pounds each)

¼ teaspoon freshly ground nutmeg

¼ cup white wine

¼ cup freshly squeezed lemon juice

¼ cup extra-virgin olive oil

½ cup dried whole-wheat bread crumbs

¼ cup coarsely chopped pistachios

¼ cup butter

Juice of 1 Seville orange (or ¼ cup orange juice
        and 2 tablespoons lemon juice)

Zest of ½ Seville orange (or 1 lemon)

1. Cut the lobsters in half lengthwise, discarding any inedible parts.

2. Preheat the broiler. Combine the nutmeg, wine, lemon juice, olive oil, and bread crumbs and spoon over the lobster halves. Place the lobsters on a baking pan and cover with aluminum foil. Broil for 10 minutes, remove the foil, and broil for 5 to 6 minutes, or until the tail meat lifts out easily. Sprinkle on the pistachios.

3. Melt the butter in a small saucepan. Add the orange juice and heat until warm.

4. Place a lobster in the center of each plate and sprinkle with the orange zest. Serve the orange butter in small dishes on the side.

To hash Lobsters

Take them out of the shells, mince them small, and put them in a pipkin with some claret wine, salt, sweet butter, grated nutmeg, slic't oranges, & some pistaches; being finely stewed, serve them on sippets, dish them, and run them over with beaten butter, slic't oranges, some cuts of paste, or lozenges of puff-paste.

THE ACCOMPLISHT COOK, 1660

Lobster Tails with Wildflowers

SERVES 4

*T*HE ACCOMPLISHT COOK lists more than twenty-one ways to prepare lobster, which was inexpensive and regularly enjoyed by the working classes in Shakespeare's time. Here, the lobster tails are steamed in floral herbal tea that imparts a lovely fragrance to the lobster. The meat is then seasoned, placed back in the tail, and covered with colorful edible summer flowers.

1 tablespoon freshly squeezed lemon juice

4 tablespoons grapeseed oil

Pinch of freshly grated nutmeg

Salt and freshly milled black pepper

2 tablespoons fresh or dried edible flower petals

4 chamomile herbal tea bags (must be 100 percent chamomile leaves)

1 mint herbal tea bag (must be 100 percent mint leaves)

4 lobster tails

½ cup assorted purple and yellow edible flowers (such as chive, borage, periwinkle, marigold, calendula, mustard flowers, or chamomile)

1 lemon, sliced

1. Whisk together the lemon juice and grapeseed oil. Add the nutmeg and season to taste with salt and pepper. Stir in the flower petals and let stand for at least 30 minutes.
2. Place the chamomile and mint tea bags in the boiling water in the bottom of a steamer. Steam the lobster tails for 7 to 10 minutes, or until the meat lifts easily out of the tail. Remove the lobster meat, reserving the shells. Roughly chop the lobster meat and toss with the vinaigrette.
3. Place a lobster tail in the center of each plate and spoon the lobster meat into the shell. Sprinkle the flowers over the lobster and arrange the lemon slices around the plates.

Scallops in Berry Glaze

SERVES 2

*T*HE ELIZABETHANS ENJOYED sweet and tart sauces and made use of various flavored vinegars in their cooking. The natural sweetness of scallops is perfectly offset here by the light tartness of fruit vinegar. This recipe is exceptionally delicious and very simple to prepare.

1 tablespoon butter

2 medium shallots, minced

½ cup fruit vinegar (raspberry, blackberry, or
    elderberry)

2 whole cloves

⅛ teaspoon mace

8 ounces sea scallops

Salt and freshly milled black pepper

¼ cup finely chopped flat-leaf parsley

¼ cup finely chopped mint

2 scallop shells, cleaned

1. Melt the butter in a sauté pan, add the shallots, and cook over low heat for 3 to 4 minutes, or until the shallots are translucent. Add the vinegar, raise the heat to medium-high, and boil for 3 minutes, or until the mixture is thickened to a glaze. Reduce the heat to medium-low, add the cloves, mace, and scallops, and cook for 1 to 2 minutes, or until the scallops are opaque and cooked through. Remove the whole cloves and season to taste with salt and pepper.

2. Combine the parsley and mint and sprinkle around the edges of the scallop shells. Spoon the scallops into the shells and top with the berry glaze.

To stew Scollops

Boil them very well in white wine, fair water, and salt, take them out of the shells, and stew them with some of the liquor, elder vinegar, two or three cloves, some large mace, and some sweet herbs choped small; being well stewed together, dish four or five of them in scollop shells and beaten butter, with the juyce of two or three oranges.

THE ACCOMPLISHT COOK, 1660

Cod Steaks with Onions and Currants

SERVES 4

*C*ARP WAS often served whole with an orange in its mouth and then plated to appear to be swimming. Many feasts occurred during Lent and on non-meat days, so fish was frequently on the menu, served roasted on a spit, baked, simmered in wine and spices, or cooked over coals.

The original recipe was also used in the soup chapter, for Seafood Soup with Rosemary Croutons (page 44). Since it was neither a true soup nor a fish dish I included both interpretations.

½ cup currants

½ cup white wine

3 tablespoons extra-virgin olive oil

2 white onions, thinly sliced

1 sprig of rosemary

3 sprigs of flat-leaf parsley

1 sprig of thyme

1 sprig of marjoram

2 whole mace blades (do not use ground, omit
    if whole is not available)

3 tablespoons wine vinegar

1 tablespoon sugar

4 cod steaks (about 7 ounces each)

Salt and freshly milled black pepper

1. Soak the currants in the wine for 1 hour.
2. Heat the olive oil in a large sauté pan, add the onions, and cook over low heat for 10 minutes, or until caramelized. Tie the rosemary, parsley, thyme, and marjoram sprigs together with kitchen string. Raise the heat to medium-high, add the tied herbs, currants, wine, mace, vinegar, sugar, and ¼ cup of water, and bring to a boil.
3. Season the cod with salt and pepper. Add the fish to the pan, reduce heat to medium, and cook for 5 minutes, or until the fish is firm and opaque. Season to taste with salt and pepper.
4. Spoon some of the onion mixture in the center of each plate and top with a cod steak.

To seeth a Carpe

First take a carpe and boyle it in water and salt, then take of the Broath and put in a little pot, then put thereto as much wine as there is broath, with rosemary, parseley, time, and margerome bounde together, and put them into the pot, & put thereto a good many of sliced Onyons, small raysins, whole Maces, a dish of butter, and a little Sugar, so that it be not to sharpe nor to sweete, and let all these seeth together: If the wine be not sharpe enough then put thereto a little Vineger, and so serve it upon soppes with broath.

THE GOOD HUSWIFES JEWELL, 1587

Mussels in Pastry

. . . Thy food shall be
The fresh-brook mussels . . .

THE TEMPEST, 1.2

*T*HIS RECIPE WAS originally a covered pie of minced mussels, but the mussels are more beautiful left whole and served in an open puff pastry. Mussels and leeks are a classic combination savored for hundreds of years. The English first noted these mollusks in the 1200s when the mussels attached themselves to the stakes seamen planted in the sand near shore. Mussels, although inexpensive in Shakespeare's day, were also prized by the rich and can be found in English cookbooks as early as 1390.

2 tablespoons butter

2 large leeks, thinly sliced (white part only)

½ cup finely chopped assorted fresh herbs (such as flat-leaf parsley, mint, tarragon, or basil)

½ teaspoon freshly ground nutmeg

½ cup white wine

½ cup freshly squeezed orange juice

2 tablespoons freshly squeezed lemon juice

Salt and freshly milled black pepper

2 pounds mussels, cleaned

2 hard-boiled egg yolks

4 large frozen puff-pastry shells, baked according to package directions

1 orange, peeled and thinly sliced

1. Melt the butter in a large sauté pan or wok. Add the leeks and sauté over medium heat for 2 minutes. Add the herbs, nutmeg, wine, orange juice, and lemon juice and season with salt and pepper. Bring the mixture to a boil and add the mussels. Cover and cook for 3 to 5 minutes, or until the mussels open.

2. Remove the mussels from the pan with a slotted spoon. Remove the mussels from the shells, discarding the shells.

3. Mash the egg yolks in a small bowl. Add 2 tablespoons of the liquid from the pan and stir until it forms a smooth paste. Add the egg mixture to the pan and cook, stirring constantly, for 2 to 3 minutes, or until the sauce thickens. Add the mussels and stir until combined.

4. Place 1 of the puff-pastry shells on each plate and spoon in the mussel mixture. Arrange the orange slices around the plates.

ORIGINAL RECIPE:

To Make a Muscle Pye

Take a peck of muscles, wash them clean, and set them a boiling in a kettle of fair water (but first let the water boil), then put them into it, give them a warm, and as soon as they are opened, take them out of the shells, stone them, and mince them with some sweet herbs, some leeks, pepper and nutmeg; mince six hard eggs and put to them, put some butter in the pye, close it up and bake it, being baked liquor it with some butter, white wine, and slices of orange.

THE ACCOMPLISHT COOK, 1660

CHAPTER EIGHT

1610 ROSE CAKES

"QUEEN ELIZABETH'S FINE CAKE"

KING JAMES BISCUITS

FOOLPROOF GOOSEBERRY "FOOLE"

BANBURY CAKE

SWEET BEETS IN PUFF PASTRY WITH CRÈME FRAÎCHE AND GINGER

"COURAGE" TART

APPLE TARTS WITH CANDIED ORANGE CRUST

BAKED APPLES WITH CINNAMON "STEMS"

CITRUS TARTS

"ORIENT RED" QUINCES

INSIDE-OUT PIE

RENAISSANCE COOKIES

CHEESECAKE "IN THE ITALIAN FASHION"

The Banquet

The setting sun, and music at the close,
As the last taste of sweets, is sweetest last . . .

KING RICHARD II, 2.1

. . . .

Since the 1300s, the nobleman's meal has ended with a sweets course called the "banquet." At first it included simple honey- and spice-sweetened wines and wafers, but by the 1500s it had expanded to include candied fruit peels (suckets), marmalades, biscuits, candy-coated spice seeds (comfits), and elaborate gingerbreads. Also by the 1500s, cream and cheese, long relegated to the tables of peasants, had regained a place at the nobility's feasts.

1610 Rose Cakes

MAKES APPROXIMATELY 36 COOKIES

> . . . That which we call a rose by any other name
> would smell as sweet . . .
>
> *ROMEO AND JULIET, 2.2*

*T*HIS RECIPE, and several others in this chapter, are from the 1610 handwritten recipe book of Sarah Longe. Mistress Longe intended the book only for her personal use and the recipes were not published during her lifetime. Holding this small, four-hundred-year-old book and reading Sarah Longe's artistic calligraphy, in faded ink, I could easily imagine Shakespeare writing on similar paper and using similar ink, perhaps even purchased at the same London stationer's shop.

½ cup butter

½ cup sugar

⅛ teaspoon ground mace

¼ cup rose syrup (available at gourmet grocers;
    or use 1 teaspoon rose water mixed with
    3 tablespoons honey and 1 tablespoon
    water)

2 tablespoons cream

2 large egg yolks

2 cups pastry flour

2 tablespoons crushed candied rose petals
    (optional)

1. Using an electric mixer on medium speed, cream the butter, sugar, mace, 2 tablespoons of the rose syrup, and the cream until light and fluffy. Beat in the egg yolks, one at a time, mixing well after each addition. Add the flour, 1 cup at a time, and mix until just incorporated.

2. Preheat the oven to 350°F. Using a cookie press in the shape of a flower, press out the cookies onto a well-buttered, nonstick baking sheet (or drop by tablespoonfuls) and bake for 10 minutes. Brush the remaining 2 tablespoons of rose syrup on the hot cookies and sprinkle with the crushed rose petals.

To make sugar Cakes

Take a pound of butter, and wash it in rose-water, and halfe a pound of sugar, and halfe a douzen spoonefulls of thicke Cream, and the yelkes of 4 Eggs, and a little mace finely beaten, and as much fine flower as it will wett, and worke it well together then roll them out very thin, and cut them with a glasse, and pricke them very thicke with a great pin, and lay them on plates, and so bake them gently.

MISTRESS SARAH LONGE HER RECEIPT BOOKE, CIRCA 1610

"Queen Elizabeth's Fine Cake"

*S*ARAH LONGE REFERS to herself as "Mistress" and not "Lady," so she was neither married to a nobleman nor of noble birth herself. However, she was probably a person of some wealth and sophistication, as one of her recipes calls for real gold as an ingredient and she mentions both Queen Elizabeth and King James I in her manuscript.

This light, not-too-sweet spice cake is wonderful one day old sliced and toasted for breakfast.

¼ cup butter

¾ cup granulated sugar

2 large egg yolks

½ teaspoon salt

¼ teaspoon ground cloves

¼ teaspoon ground mace

½ teaspoon freshly ground nutmeg

3 cups unbleached flour, sifted

1 cup cream

½ cup currants

¼ cup raisins

1 cup confectioners' sugar

2 tablespoons rose syrup (available at gourmet
    grocers; or use 1 teaspoon rose water mixed
    with 1½ tablespoons honey)

1. Beat the butter and granulated sugar with an electric mixer on medium speed until well mixed. Add the egg yolks one at a time, mixing well after each addition. Add the salt, cloves, mace, and nutmeg and mix well. Alternate mixing in the flour and cream, beating on low speed after each addition until well blended. Stir in the currants and raisins.

2. Preheat the oven to 350°F. Form the dough into a 3 by 16-inch cigar shape on a well-greased parchment-lined baking sheet. Bake the loaf for 25 minutes, or until golden brown and a knife inserted in the center comes out clean.

3. Place the confectioners' sugar and rose syrup in a small bowl and mix until smooth. Spread the icing over the cooled loaf.

4. Cut in 1-inch-thick slices and serve immediately. (Any leftovers can be made into biscotti by slicing them ¾ inch thick and baking for 10 minutes at 350°F.)

Sarah Longe notes, "This is called Queen Elizabeth's fine Cake." The queen's sweet tooth, like that of her countrymen, was legendary throughout Europe. A German traveler, Paul Hentzner, visiting England in 1598, wrote a description of the then-sixty-five-year-old monarch: "very majestic; her Face oblong, fair, but wrinkled; her Eyes small, yet black and pleasant; her Nose a little hooked; her Lips narrow; her Teeth black; a defect the English seem subject to, from their too great use of sugar."

The Elizabethans did try to take care of their teeth, and cookbooks of the time contained assorted recipes for mouthwash and toothpaste. Unfortunately the main ingredient was always sugar!

King James Biscuits

According to Mistress Sarah Longe, writing in her personal recipe book in about 1610, "King James, and his Queene [had] eaten with much liking" these delicious sconelike biscuits.

The Folger Shakespeare Library in Washington, D.C., houses Sarah Longe's cookbook and an extensive collection of manuscripts, published books, and documents from Shakespeare's lifetime, including some signed by Queen Elizabeth I and others signed by King James I, her successor. One bite explains why King James and his queen enjoyed these light, tasty scones with their tangy combination of caraway and aniseeds.

7 large egg yolks

3 tablespoons rose water

1 cup sugar

5 cups pastry flour

4 large egg whites

1 teaspoon caraway seeds

1 teaspoon aniseeds

1. Using an electric mixer on high speed, beat the egg yolks, rose water, and sugar for 2 minutes. Add 1 cup of flour and mix for 2 minutes. Add another cup of flour and mix for 1 minute. Reduce the mixer speed to low, add another cup of flour, and mix for 2 minutes. In a separate bowl, whip the egg whites to soft peaks. Add another cup of flour, the caraway, aniseed, and the egg whites to the batter and mix for 2 minutes. Add the remaining cup of flour and mix until smooth and elastic. (If the dough is too thick for your mixer, knead in the last addition of flour.)

2. Preheat the oven to 350°F. Drop the dough, 2 tablespoons at a time, onto a greased cookie sheet and bake for 15 minutes, or until light golden brown.

Shakespeare did not want his plays published for sale in bookshops, as he earned his living by having the works performed in theaters to a paying audience. Several years after his death, however, friends and actors who wanted to "keep the memory of so worthy a friend and Fellow alive" fortunately published the majority of Shakespeare's works. It is thanks to them that we have all his plays in print today.

Shakespeare wrote his plays and sonnets in his own hand, yet none of the original pages have survived. After writing a play, he would send the pages to the printer so copies could be created for the actors. After setting the type, the printer, having no further use for them, would throw away the originals.

Foolproof Gooseberry "Foole"

*G*OOSEBERRY FOOLE is still one of the more popular English desserts. Since berries are themselves so fragrant, I omitted the rose water suggested as an ingredient in the original recipe. This
is a light, tart version of the traditional "foole," much loved by Shakespeare and his contemporaries.

6 ounces gooseberries, husked (or any berry)

3 tablespoons granulated sugar

Dash of mace (or nutmeg)

1 cup cream

1 tablespoon turbinado sugar (or light brown sugar)

1. Set aside 4 gooseberries. Place the remaining gooseberries in a small saucepan of boiling water and cook
   for 5 minutes, discarding any loose skins. Drain the berries, put in a small bowl, and mash with a fork.
   Add the granulated sugar and mace and cool to room temperature.
2. Whip the cream with a whisk or an electric mixer until soft peaks form.
3. Divide the gooseberry mixture among 4 small serving glasses and top with some of the whipped cream.
   Slice the reserved gooseberries and arrange the slices over the whipped cream. Sprinkle with the
   turbinado sugar and serve immediately.

ORIGINAL RECIPE:

To make a Gooseberry Foole

Take two handfulls of greene Gooseberies, and pricke them, then scald them very soft,
and poure the water from them very cleane, and breake them very small, and season
them with rose-water, and sugar, and then take a quart of Creame, or butter, and put in
a little mace, and sett it on the fire (letting it boyle), and then take it of, and take out
the Mace, and poure it into the Gooseberies, and stirre it about, and lett it stand till it
bee cold, and then eate it.

MISTRESS SARAH LONGE HER RECEIPT BOOKE, CIRCA 1610

Gingerbread houses have been a holiday favorite since before Shakespeare's birth. Castles and other buildings constructed of sweet dough adorned the dessert tables of noblemen in the Middle Ages.

Gingerbread men too have their origins in the Middle Ages, when they were made to represent saints and were eaten on the given saint's patron day.

A version of Chinese fortune cookies was also in existence in England in Shakespeare's time. Elizabethan cookbooks contained recipes for baking poems into tiny walnut-shaped pastry shells.

An I had but one penny in the world, thou
shouldst have it to buy gingerbread . . .
LOVE'S LABOUR'S LOST, 5.1

Banbury Cake

SERVES 10 TO 12

You Banbury cheese!

THE MERRY WIVES OF WINDSOR, 1.1

$\mathcal{T}$HE TOWN OF Banbury, England, was known for its cheese and cakes in Shakespeare's day. Published by Gervase Markham in 1615, this is probably the first recorded recipe for Banbury Cake. The original was an un-iced yeast cake with a center section of currants. In this version, baking powder is used to produce a lighter cake, and a warm currant purée is served on the side. For variety, you might substitute dried cherries, which were also available then, for the currants.

¼ cup butter, softened

1 cup plus 2 tablespoons sugar

1 large egg

1 large egg white

½ cup milk

¼ cup cream

1½ teaspoons baking powder

⅛ teaspoon ground cloves

½ teaspoon ground mace

½ teaspoon ground nutmeg

⅛ teaspoon ground cinnamon

½ teaspoon salt

1¾ cups cake flour

¾ cup currants

1. Preheat the oven to 350°F. Place the butter, 1 cup of the sugar, the whole egg, egg white, milk, cream, baking powder, cloves, mace, nutmeg, cinnamon, and salt in a large bowl. Using an electric mixer on medium speed, beat for 1 to 2 minutes, or until completely combined. Add the flour, ½ cup at a time, beating on low speed after each addition, until the flour is just incorporated.

2. Pour the batter into a greased and floured 9-inch round cake pan. Bake for 30 minutes, or until the cake springs back when touched and a knife comes out clean. Cool and cut into 10 to 12 wedges.

3. Simmer the currants, the remaining 2 tablespoons of sugar, and 1 cup of water for about 20 minutes, or until most of the liquid has evaporated. Purée until smooth.

4. Place a slice of cake in the center of each plate and spoon some of the warm purée on the side.

Sweet Beets in Puff Pastry with Crème Fraîche and Ginger

SERVES 6

*A*LTHOUGH THIS RECIPE from Lombardy, Italy, was originally intended as a sweet side dish for savory roasted meats, I thought it might make an unusual dessert. Instead of mixing the cheese and ginger with the beets as suggested in the original, I use them in the toppings as crème fraîche and crystallized ginger.

 6 small golden or red beets, peeled and
  finely grated
 2 tablespoons honey
 2 tablespoons butter, melted
 ¼ teaspoon ground cinnamon
 1 package frozen puff-pastry shells (6 per package)
 ½ cup crème fraîche
 2 tablespoons minced crystallized ginger

1. Preheat the oven to 425°F. Combine the beets, honey, butter, and cinnamon in an oven-safe container. Mix well and let stand for 5 minutes. Bake, covered with aluminum foil, for 15 minutes. Remove from the oven and drain any excess liquid from the pan.
2. Bake the puff-pastry shells according to package directions.
3. Spoon the beet mixture into the puff-pastry shells and top with a dollop of crème fraîche. Sprinkle the crystallized ginger over the beets and crème fraîche and serve immediately.

ORIGINAL RECIPE:

To make Lumdardy tarts

Take Beets, chop them small, and put to them grated bread and cheese, and mingle them wel in the chopping, take a few Currans, and a dish of sweet Butter, & melt it then stir al these in the Butter, together with three yolks of Egs, Synamon, ginger, and sugar, and make your Tart as large as you will, and fill it with the stuffe, bake it, and serve it in.

THE GOOD HUSWIVES HANDMAIDE FOR THE KITCHIN, 1594

In Shakespeare's time, sugar was considered an aphrodisiac and the banquet was specifically designed to "moveth pleasure and lust of the body."

Sweets were often served on plates called "roundels" or "banqueting dishes," which had an image or poem on them. Often these poems contained sexual innuendos and double entendres.

Bring in the banquet quickly; wine enough
Cleopatra's health to drink.
ANTONY AND CLEOPATRA, 1.2

"Courage" Tart

SERVES 8

I WAS INTRIGUED by the recipe title "To make a Tarte that is a courage to a man or woman," found in a 1587 cookbook. The courage referred to is sexual prowess. Several of the ingredients, including sweet potatoes and wine, were considered aphrodisiacs back then. You will notice, however, that another aphrodisiac ingredient, sparrow brains, was purposely omitted in this modern version!

1 large sweet potato, peeled and diced

2 cups white dessert wine (such as Muscat)

2 quinces or apples, peeled, cored, and diced

3 dates, pitted and chopped

½ recipe of Renaissance Dough (page 239)

2 tablespoons light brown sugar

⅛ teaspoon ground cinnamon

⅛ teaspoon ground ginger

Pinch of ground cloves

⅛ teaspoon ground mace

2 tablespoons butter, softened

4 large egg yolks

1 teaspoon rose water

2 large egg whites

1. Place the sweet potato and wine in a small saucepan over medium-low heat and simmer for 10 minutes. Add the quinces and dates and simmer for 25 minutes, or until the quinces are tender. (If the mixture becomes too dry, add 1 or 2 tablespoons of wine.) Purée until smooth.

2. Preheat the oven to 350°F. Roll out the Renaissance Dough to ⅛ inch thick on a floured work surface. Press the dough into a pie pan and trim off any excess.

3. Place the sweet potato mixture in a large bowl. Add the brown sugar, cinnamon, ginger, cloves, mace, and butter and stir until well combined. Beat the egg yolks and rose water in a small bowl, add to the filling, and mix well. Whisk the egg whites to stiff peaks and gently fold into the filling. Pour the filling into the piecrust and bake for 1 hour, or until the center springs back when lightly pressed.

To make a Tarte that is a courage to a man or woman

Take two Quinces and two or three Burre rootes, and a potaton, and pare your Potaton and scrape your rootes and put them into a quart of wine, and let them boyle till they be tender, and put in an ounce of Dates, and when they be boyled tender, draw them through a Strainer, Wine and all, and then putte in the yolkes of eight Egges, and the brains of three or foure cocke Sparrowes, and Straine them into the other and a little Rose water, and seeth them all with Sugar, Synamon and Ginger, and Cloves and Mace, and put in a little Sweete butter, and set it upon a chafingdishe of coles, betweene two platter, and so let it boyle till it be something bigge.

THE GOOD HUSWIFES JEWELL, 1587

In the quote below, Shakespeare mentions three of the most popular aphrodisiacs of the time: sweet potatoes, musk-flavored candy called kissing-comfits, and candied eringo root. The audience would have surely laughed at the line's bawdy suggestiveness.

One in five Elizabethan brides was already pregnant on her wedding day. Shakespeare's own bride, Anne Hathaway, gave birth to their daughter Susanna only six months after the wedding. Apparently neither Anne nor Shakespeare needed this pie!

Let the sky rain potatoes; . . . hail kissing-
comfits, and snow eringoes . . .
THE MERRY WIVES OF WINDSOR, 5.5

Apple Tarts with Candied Orange Crust

SERVES 4

> What, up and down, carv'd like an apple-tart?
>
> *THE TAMING OF THE SHREW, 4.3*

APPLE PIE, and even apples, are an English contribution to the American table. The first British settlers brought apple seeds and apple pie recipes with them to America. This original recipe was for apple pie mixed with candied orange slices. Instead, I incorporated candied peel into a free-form crust and topped the apples with an orange glaze for a slight twist on an old favorite.

¼ cup freshly squeezed orange juice

1 tablespoon rose water

¼ cup sugar

¼ cup Candied Citrus Peel (page 237)

2 cooking apples, peeled, cored, and sliced
    ¼ inch thick

2 tablespoons honey

½ teaspoon ground cinnamon

¼ teaspoon ground ginger

1 tablespoon butter, melted

½ recipe of Renaissance Dough (page 239)

1 large egg, beaten

1. Bring the orange juice, rose water, 2 tablespoons of the sugar, and 1 tablespoon of the citrus peel to a boil. Simmer for 3 to 5 minutes, or until slightly thickened.

2. Toss the apples with the remaining 2 tablespoons of sugar, the honey, cinnamon, ginger, and butter.

3. Preheat the oven to 375°F. Roll out the Renaissance Dough into an 8 by 10-inch rectangle on a floured work surface. Press the remaining citrus peel into the dough. Cut the dough into four 4 by 5-inch rectangles and place on a greased or parchment-lined baking sheet. Lay the apple slices in a tight row in the center of the dough and pinch up the sides of the dough to form the edge crust. Brush the dough with the egg. Brush the apples with the glaze and bake for 25 minutes, or until the crust is golden brown and the apples are tender.

The word *dessert* comes from the Middle French *desservir,* meaning to remove the table. The following lines from *Romeo and Juliet* refer to the dancing and entertainment that were to take place after the feast tables were removed.

Come, musicians, play.
A hall, a hall! give room! and foot it, girls.
More light, you knaves; and turn
the tables up . . .
ROMEO AND JULIET, **1.5**

Baked Apples with Cinnamon "Stems"

HE CINNAMON STICKS peeking out of the center of the apples look like little stems, making this an especially beautiful dessert. Many recipes from Shakespeare's day call for butter. Considered beneficial to health, it was even rubbed on a baby's gums to ease teething. An old English proverb, "Butter is Gold in the morning, and silver at noon, and lead at night," refers to when butter is freshest and best digested.

24 whole cloves

12 very small, sweet apples, peeled and cored

12 dates, pitted and quartered

¼ cup Candied Citrus Peel, minced (page 237)

2 tablespoons orange liqueur (such as Cointreau)

½ cup brown sugar

¼ cup butter

Twelve 2-inch-long cinnamon sticks

Zest of 1 orange

1. Preheat the oven to 350°F. Grease an 8- or 9-inch round baking pan. Press 2 whole cloves into the outside of each apple and place the apples upright in the baking pan.

2. Combine the dates, citrus peel, liqueur, and brown sugar in a small bowl. Spoon some of the date mixture into the center of each apple. Place a thin pat of butter on the top of each apple and press a cinnamon stick into the center, leaving a ½-inch "stem" exposed. Cover the pan with aluminum foil and bake for 20 minutes. Remove the aluminum foil and bake for 30 minutes, or until the apples are tender. Top with long strips of orange zest before serving.

Fruit such as apples, cherries, figs, apricots, and berries were served both fresh and dried at the end of a meal. Blackberries were apparently so abundant in England that Shakespeare used them to denote something of little worth, as in the lines "if reasons were as plentiful as blackberries" (*King Henry IV,* Part I, 2.4) and "is not proved worth a blackberry" (*Troilus and Cressida,* 5.4).

My news shall be the fruit
to that great feast.
HAMLET, 2.2

Citrus Tarts

SERVES 6

Here's the challenge, read it: I warrant there's vinegar and pepper in't.

TWELFTH NIGHT, 3.4

I DOUBT YOUR GUESTS will guess that these refreshing tarts contain both pepper and vinegar, two flavors not ordinarily associated with dessert. Peppercorns, popular since the time of ancient Greece and Rome, were often included in sweet dishes in Shakespeare's day. In Medieval times this valuable spice was traded as money. "Peppercorn rent," a legal term for a symbolic or nominal payment, is still used in England today.

> 4 large navel oranges
>
> 3 lemons
>
> 2 tablespoons butter
>
> ½ teaspoon freshly ground five-color peppercorns
>
> 3 teaspoons minced fresh ginger
>
> 3 tablespoons sugar
>
> ½ cup white wine
>
> 2 tablespoons verjuice
>
> 1 tablespoon honey
>
> 15 ready-made tiny phyllo tart shells (1-inch
>
> diameter)

1. Using a vegetable peeler, cut the peel from the oranges and lemons, removing any of the white pith. Soak the peels for 10 minutes in cold water. Drain and coarsely chop the peels.
2. Melt the butter in a medium nonreactive saucepan. Add the chopped peels, peppercorns, ginger, sugar, and wine, and bring to a boil. Reduce the heat and simmer for 30 minutes. Allow the mixture to cool to room temperature and stir in the verjuice and honey.
3. Spoon the filling into the tart shells and serve.

To bake a Citron pye

Take your Citrone, pare it and slice it in peeces, and boyle it with grose Pepper and Ginger, and so laye it in your Paste with Butter, and when it is almost baked, put thereto Vineger, Butter, and Sugar, and let it stande in the Oven a while and soke.

THE GOOD HUSWIFES JEWELL, 1587

"Orient Red" Quinces

SERVES 6

And that same dew, which sometime on the buds
Was wont to swell like round and orient pearls,
Stood now within the pretty flouriets' eyes
Like tears that did their own disgrace bewail.

A MIDSUMMER NIGHT'S DREAM, 4.1

*O*RIENT," MEANING GLOWING, was the apt description in the original recipe for this lovely dessert that can be made with quinces or apples. Slowly cooking the fruit whole in spiced wine produces slices that are bright red on the outside but still white in the center. The fruit was too pretty to put into a piecrust as suggested in 1631, so here it is simply sliced and served with the spiced wine syrup on the side. This syrup is also delicious served with fresh strawberries.

2 large quinces or tart apples, peeled and cored

2½ cups red wine

4 whole cloves

½ cup dark brown sugar

One 2-inch piece of cinnamon stick

1. Place the quinces, wine, cloves, brown sugar, and cinnamon in a small saucepan and simmer for 20 to 30 minutes, or until just tender. Remove the quinces from the pan and cook the liquid for 20 minutes, or until thick and syrupy.

2. Slice each quince in half and cut into ⅛-inch-thick slices. Spoon a little of the syrup in the center of each plate and arrange the quince slices around the syrup to form a flower.

Inside-Out Pie

SERVES 6

They call for dates and quinces in the pastry.

ROMEO AND JULIET, 4.4

ERE'S AN APPLE PIE with a twist! The fruit forms the crust, while the bread is the filling. The original recipe, entitled "A bakte Pudding after the Italian Fashion," calls for suet and bone marrow, but since the dish originated in Italy, I felt reasonably justified in substituting Italian prosciutto for those ingredients. The original recipe's charming baking instructions—"If the oven be too hot, it will burn, if it be too cold, it will be too heavy"—gave me a new appreciation for our modern oven thermostats.

9 slices of firm white bread, crusts removed

2 large eggs

1 large egg white

1 tablespoon butter, melted

¼ cup golden raisins

6 dates, pitted and chopped

Pinch of ground cloves

⅛ teaspoon ground mace

⅛ teaspoon freshly ground nutmeg

Pinch of salt

½ cup cream

½ cup milk

¼ cup minced prosciutto

1 tart apple, peeled, cored, and thinly sliced

1 tablespoon superfine sugar

1. Cut the bread into ½-inch cubes. Place the eggs and egg white in a large bowl and beat very well. Add the butter, raisins, dates, cloves, mace, nutmeg, salt, cream, milk, and prosciutto and mix well. Fold the bread into the mixture and let stand for 15 minutes, or until the liquid is absorbed. (If the mixture looks dry, add a bit more milk.)

2. Preheat the oven to 350°F. Grease a 9-inch springform pan. Starting in the center, shingle the apple slices in a spiral around the bottom and up the sides of the pan. Add the bread mixture, taking care not to disturb the apples. Bake for 30 minutes, or until light golden brown. Invert onto a large plate, sprinkle with superfine sugar, and serve immediately. If desired, the pie can be broiled for a few seconds to caramelize the sugar.

Groundlings, audience members with the least expensive tickets, had to stand on the ground in front of the stage while the most elite, expensive seats were those highest up. As Shakespeare refers to in this quote, the groundlings were all too happy to munch on any leftovers the rich tossed down.

These are the youths that thunder at a
playhouse, and fight for bitten apples . . .
KING HENRY VIII, 5.4

Renaissance Cookies

MAKES 36 COOKIES

> The daintiest last, to make the end most sweet . . .
>
> *KING RICHARD II*, 1.3

IN THE ORIGINAL recipe the cookies were topped with either small red or white sugar-coated candies, called "muskedines," or sugar-coated fennel and caraway seeds, a frequent "bisket" topping. The Elizabethans would also "scrape on fine sugar." Sugar sold in hard bricks or cones had to be scraped loose in those days.

In this modern version the cookies are topped with a cutout from the dough, which keeps the almond-flavored spinach filling moist. Once you taste these delicate cookies you'll know why this four-hundred-year-old recipe is still made today in many regions of Italy.

1 cup butter, softened

¾ cup granulated sugar

1 large egg, beaten

¼ cup white dessert wine (such as Muscat)

¼ teaspoon salt

2 cups whole-wheat pastry flour

2 cups white pastry flour

10 ounces fresh baby spinach, cooked and

    well drained

1 large egg yolk, beaten

4 ounces almond paste

3 teaspoons cream

3 tablespoons superfine sugar

1. Cream the butter and granulated sugar until light and fluffy. Add the egg, wine, and ⅛ teaspoon of the salt and mix well. Add the whole-wheat and white flours, a little at a time, and mix until completely incorporated.

2. Purée the spinach. Add the egg yolk, almond paste, cream, and remaining ⅛ teaspoon salt and purée for 1 minute, or until the almond paste has dissolved. Mix in up to 3 tablespoons of the superfine sugar to

taste. (Some almond pastes already contain sugar.) Simmer the mixture over very low heat, stirring frequently, for 15 minutes, or until very thick.

3. Preheat the oven to 350°F. Roll out the cookie dough to $\frac{1}{8}$ inch thick on a floured work surface and cut thirty-six 2-inch circles and thirty-six $\frac{3}{4}$- to 1-inch cutouts of the desired shape (such as cloverleaf or diamond). Spread about 1 tablespoon of the spinach mixture onto each circle and top with a cutout. Bake on a lightly greased cookie sheet for 20 minutes.

ORIGINAL RECIPE:

Other made Dish of spinach in Paste baked

Boil spinage as beforesaid, being tender boil'd, drain it in a cullender, chop it small, and strain it with half a pound of almond-paste, three or four yolks of eggs, half a grain of musk, three or four spoonfuls of cream, a quartern of fine sugar, and a little salt; then bake it on a sheet of paste on a dish without a cover, in a very soft oven, being fine and green baked, stick it with preserved barberries, or strow on red and white biskets, or red and white muskedines, and scrape on fine sugar.

THE ACCOMPLISHT COOK, 1660

Cheesecake "in the Italian Fashion"

SERVES 6 TO 8

*T*HIS ELIZABETHAN RECIPE, adapted from Italy, calls for "morning milk cheese or better." I was curious how an Elizabethan chef would have prepared a classic Italian Renaissance dish. Unlike most Italian cheesecakes of the time, the English version had a crust. This modern version creates a creamy pistachio-studded cheesecake with a quick and simple grated biscotti crust.

15 ounces whole-milk ricotta

8 ounces cottage cheese (4 percent milk fat)

1 large egg

½ cup sugar

¼ teaspoon ground cinnamon

⅛ teaspoon ground mace

¼ cup coarsely chopped unsalted pistachios

7 almond biscotti

1. Blend the ricotta, cottage cheese, and egg in a food processor until very smooth. Add the sugar, cinnamon, and mace and mix until smooth. Stir in the pistachios.

2. Preheat the oven to 300°F. Grate 6 of the biscotti into the bottom of a 9-inch pie pan and pour in the cheese mixture. Bake for 1½ hours. Grate the remaining biscotti over the cheesecake and refrigerate for at least 1 hour before serving.

Chocolate and vanilla, two flavors highly associated with desserts today, are not found in this chapter. Shakespeare never tasted either one. The Spanish discovered chocolate in Mexico and South America and it wasn't introduced into England until well after Shakespeare's lifetime.

Vanilla, another dessert classic indigenous to Mexico, wasn't imported to Europe until the 1700s.

Shakespeare never drank the prototypical English beverage, tea. He never drank coffee, either. No Elizabethan did. Tea and coffee were not introduced into that country until well after Shakespeare's time.

I will make an end of my dinner;
There's pippins and cheese to come.
THE MERRY WIVES OF WINDSOR, 1.2

CHAPTER NINE

CANDIED CITRUS PEEL
RENAISSANCE DOUGH
RENAISSANCE STOCK

Basics

Sweets with sweets war not, joy delights in joy.

SONNET 8

. . . .

Delightes for Ladies, Sir Hugh Plat's 1603 cookbook, is the source for all the recipes in this chapter. Plat begins his cookbook with a charming introduction written in verse that illuminates his gentle nature. Protesting the ongoing fighting between nations, he writes:

LET PIERCING BULLETS TURNE TO SUGAR BALS,
THE SPANISH FEARE IS HUSHT AND ALL THEIR RAGE,
OF MARMELADE AND PASTE OF GENUA,
OF MUSKED SUGARS I INTEND TO WRIGHT,
AFFORDING TO EACH LADY HER DELIGHT.

Sir Hugh Plat prefers the pen to weapons.

I SCORNE TO WRITE WITH COPPRES, OR WITH GALL,
BARBARIAN CANES ARE NOW BECOME MY QUILLS,
ROSEWATER IS THE INKE I WRITE WITHALL:

In another line he speaks with hope that his era will be remembered for its decorative marzipan sculptures instead of its public display of beheadings.

EMPALINGS, NOW ADEW, LUSH MARCHPAINE WALS
ARE STRONG ENOUGH, AND BEST BEFITS OUR AGE.

Candied Citrus Peel

MAKES ABOUT 1 CUP

> You say true:
> Why, what a candy deal of courtesy
> This fawning greyhound then did proffer me!
>
> *KING HENRY IV, PART I, 1.3*

*O*RANGES AND LEMONS were expensive, so people took care not to waste any part of the fruit. Before becoming enchanted with Plat's book, I had never candied fruit peels. It's easy and the results are superior to the store-bought varieties available at the holidays. Add them to muffin or cake recipes, stuffing, soups, stews, or, finely minced, try them sprinkled on buttered toast for a change from marmalade.

3 oranges

3 lemons

2 cups granulated sugar

½ cup superfine sugar

1. Using a sharp knife or vegetable peeler, cut the peel from the oranges and lemons, removing any of the white pith. Soak the peels in cold water for 10 minutes. Discard the water and rinse the peels under cold running water. Place the peels in a saucepan and cover with cold water. Bring to a boil and cook for 1 minute. Drain and rinse under cold running water. Repeat the process two more times, rinsing well after boiling.

2. Preheat the oven to 200°F. Bring ¼ cup of water, the granulated sugar, and the peels to a boil for 5 minutes. Remove from the heat and cool in the liquid. Drain in a colander and let dry slightly. Place a sheet of parchment on a baking pan. Sprinkle the superfine sugar onto the parchment and toss the peels in the sugar until coated. Discard the excess sugar. Bake the sugared peels for 1 hour, or until dry. Store in an airtight container for up to 1 month.

To candy Orenge pilles

Take your Orenge pilles after they bee preserved, then take fine sugar and Rosewater, &
boile it to the height of Manus Christi, then draw it through your sugar, then lay them
on the bottome of a sieve, and drie them in an oven after you have drawne bread, and
they will be candied.

DELIGHTES FOR LADIES, 1603

In Plat's original recipe he explains how to blanch peels, exactly as we do today, with three
changes of boiling water. The *Manus Christi,* or "hand of Christ," referred to in the recipe was a
candy popular in Shakespeare's day.

Renaissance Dough

MAKES 1 DOUBLE CRUST

*T*HIS DOUGH, or "paste" as it was called, is perfect for a two-crust sweet or savory pie. In Shakespeare's day, after baking, the top crust on dessert pies was often replaced with a separately baked, highly ornate top crust of multicolored preserves or sugars with intricate designs.

Of course, you may use store-bought ready-to-use or frozen crusts for any of the recipes in this book calling for Renaissance Dough. Nowadays, with so many good ready-made options available, you don't need to lie "guiltily awake" (*King Richard III*, 5.3) if you don't want to bother with the fuss of making your own dough.

2 cups sifted loosely packed pastry flour (8 ounces)

1/2 teaspoon salt

1 large egg, beaten, cold

1/2 cup butter, cut in small cubes, cold

Mix the flour, 1/2 cup ice-cold water, the salt, and egg together on a cold surface until crumbly. Flatten the dough with a rolling pin and place one quarter of the butter cubes on the dough. (Keep the remaining butter refrigerated until ready to use.) Roll the butter into the dough, fold the dough over, and roll again. Repeat the process 3 more times until all the butter is incorporated. Cover the dough in plastic wrap and refrigerate for at least 1 hour.

ORIGINAL RECIPE:

To make a puffe paste

Take a quart of the finest flower and the whites of three egges, and the yolkes of two, and a little colde water and so make it into perfect paste, then drive it with a rouling pin abroade, then put on small peeces of butter as big as Nuts upon it, then folde it over, then drive it abroad againe, then put small peeces of butter upon it as you did before, doe this tenne times, always folding the paste and putting butter between everie folde. You may convey anie prettie forced dish, as Florentine, Cherry, tarte, rice, or pippen, & c. between two sheets of that paste.

DELIGHTES FOR LADIES, 1603

Renaissance Stock

*T*HE DRIED FRUIT imparts a delicate sweetness to this lovely stock. Sweet is a theme throughout Sir Hugh Plat's *Delightes for Ladies*, which includes recipes for making sugar animals, rock candy, and marzipan and for preserving clusters of grapes by placing the stems into apples.

The book also contains nonedible recipes—such as a "handwater of Scotland" made with thyme, lavender, and rosemary—as well as outlandish advice to keep the skin clear and blemish-free by rubbing on the burned, ground jawbone of a hog.

4½ pounds chicken parts (necks, backs,
    wings, giblets)

1 lamb shank (about 8 ounces)

2 sprigs of rosemary

2 bay leaves

3 sprigs of mint

4 sprigs of flat-leaf parsley

1 whole mace

2 onions, peeled and quartered

1 cup white wine

½ cup ground blanched almonds

8 dates, pitted and chopped

½ cup currants

Salt and freshly milled black pepper

Place the chicken and shank bone in a large pot. Add 2¾ quarts of water and bring to a boil. Skim the impurities that rise to the top. Add the rosemary, bay leaves, mint, parsley, mace, and onions and simmer for 30 minutes. Add the wine, almonds, dates, and currants and simmer for 1 hour, periodically skimming any impurities that rise to the top. Strain through a fine-mesh sieve. Season to taste with salt and pepper.

Sir Hugh Plat was not only a chef, but also a chemist, inventor, and even magician, as shown in *The Jewel House of Art and Nature,* another of his books. Knowledge of chemistry is apparent in his instructions on changing ink color with lemon juice and on drying parsnips to extract their sugar. The book includes tricks on how to make an egg stand on end, how to hold a hot rod in a bare hand, and how to make a variegated crystal ring to spy on an opponent's playing cards. The book also describes invention ideas that eventually earned him a knighthood from King James I.

And of this book this learning mayst thou taste.
SONNET 77

CHAPTER TEN

Feasting and Bills of Fare

A good digestion to you all: and once more I show'r

a welcome on ye; welcome all.

KING HENRY VIII, 1.4

. . . .

With fewer entertainment options than we have today, a dinner feast was an especially significant event in Shakespeare's time. Hosts reveled in displaying status, making
new alliances, and repaying debts through elaborate multidish courses and fantastical
culinary presentations.

Feasts with fifty or more separate dishes were common for special events, but
guests were not expected to try all fifty dishes. The assortment of dishes was presented
so that each person could find something he or she liked. In 1617, Frayn Moryson, a
travel writer, wrote of this English custom, "The English tables are not furnished with
many dishes, all for one mans diet, but severaly for many mens appetite, . . . that each
may take what hee likes."

Following are highlights of how people entertained in Shakespeare's day with
hints on how to give Shakespeare-themed dinners, buffets, and parties.

CASTING CALL

. . . . .

. . . FIND THOSE PERSONS OUT
WHOSE NAMES ARE WRITTEN THERE, AND TO THEM SAY,
MY HOUSE AND WELCOME ON THEIR PLEASURE STAY.

Romeo and Juliet, 1.2

AS THERE WAS NO MAIL SYSTEM IN SHAKESPEARE'S DAY, MESSENGERS WERE SENT TO personally invite each guest to a feast.

For your own modern feast you might like to copy one of the following sample invitations. You can re-create them in calligraphy or on a computer. Staining the paper with tea or burning its edges adds a theatrical aged effect. Closing the invitation envelope with sealing wax is another nice Elizabethan touch. Seals with initials and sealing wax can be purchased at fine stationery stores.

BRUSH UP YOUR SHAKESPEARE
START QUOTING HIM NOW.

—Cole Porter

Celebrate Shakespeare's Birthday!

———

Dress according to thy whim!

PARTY GIVEN BY:

ADDRESS:

To be held on:

At   o'clock

THE FAVOR OF YOUR REPLY IS REQUESTED

Please phone: *By:*

———

YOU ARE INVITED TO A
SHAKESPEAREAN DINNER PARTY

———————

REVEL AND FEAST IT AT MY HOUSE.
THE COMEDY OF ERRORS

AT THE HOME OF:

ON:

ADDRESS:

Please RSVP by:

TO:

GIVE ME YOUR HAND;

WE MUST NEEDS DINE TOGETHER.

—Timon of Athens

YOUR NAME & ADDRESS

EAT WITH US TO-NIGHT,

THE CHARGE AND THANKING

SHALL BE FOR ME.

—All's Well That Ends Well

Date, Time, and RSVP info

YOU MIGHT HAVE THRUST HIM

AND ALL HIS APPAREL INTO AN EEL-SKIN.

—King Henry VIII, Part II

WEAR ACTOR'S BLACK

SEATING

. . . . .

DURING THE CLASSICAL PERIOD, IT WAS BELIEVED IDEAL FOR A PARTY TO INCLUDE no fewer than three guests, the number of the Graces, and no more than twelve, equaling the Muses. Although the Greek ideal was known in Shakespeare's time, Renaissance dinners often included many more guests. Large feasts got so out of hand that in Italy special laws were enacted that specified the number of guests allowed based on the host's social rank.

Seating was very carefully orchestrated in Shakespeare's day with the hierarchy for table placement of a duke, marquese, earl, bishop, viscount, baron, or knight well defined. A page would escort each diner to his or her place based on a printed master seating list. All seating was assigned by social position and rank.

For your own feast, you might make place cards from color copies of sixteenth- or seventeenth-century paintings. Or use postcards of paintings, which are available at most museum gift shops. Scrolls made from parchmentlike stationery can also serve as place cards. Each scroll can include a different Shakespeare quotation or historical food fact for your guest to read aloud.

Knowing whom to invite and, even more important, where to seat the guests you have invited is often the key difference between a wonderfully noisy and chatty dinner party and an average gathering.

To stimulate conversation, seat couples and friends who know each other well at opposite ends of the table. Place people with similar hobbies, not necessarily similar occupations, near each other. For example, rather than seating two attorneys together, place the mountain-biking litigator near the artist who hikes.

In planning your guest list don't shy away from including someone you just met. What better way to get acquainted than in your own home with a group of your friends? Even if it turns out that you don't have anything in common, one of your other friends might. Consider including a relative on your dinner-party guest list. It is often pleasantly surprising how different someone can be away from the rest of the clan.

SCENERY AND PROPS

· · · · ·

LIGHTING

The sun, firelight, and candles were the only sources of illumination in Elizabethan England. A room lit by candles is dramatic for a modern party. Beeswax candles have a lovely glow and add a pleasant fragrance to the room.

LINENS AND TABLEWARE

As guests entered the dining hall, they washed their hands in scented and flowered water provided by the host. Guests would find very large, plain white cloth napkins at their places to use during dinner and to wrap leftovers to take home. Women were expected to place the napkin on their lap, men to tie it over the left shoulder or over their left arm.

In *Murrells Two Books of Cookerie and Carving,* the butler or pantler is advised to "lay the cloths, wipe the boorde cleane . . . then set your Salt on the right side where your Soveraigne shall sit."

Judging from sixteenth- and seventeenth-century paintings of feasts, tablecloths were almost always white. It remained the typical color for table coverings until the end of the Victorian era. If you prefer to create a more fanciful setting, use the colors popular then: gold, burgundy, and royal blue. A velvet cloth, a tapestry, or even a Chinese rug might be a possible table covering for your modern Elizabethan party.

Costly china and ceramic plates and dishes were not yet common in Shakespeare's day and instead wooden, pewter, or silver plates were used.

I DRINK TO TH' GENERAL JOY O' TH' WHOLE TABLE . . .

Macbeth, 3.4

Raising one's glass to the health of another guest, especially of an esteemed lady at the table, was common in Elizabethan England, and various etiquette books suggested apt sayings. Pieces of toast have been added to drinks since the Middle Ages to improve the beverages' flavor, and it is from that practice that we derive the expression "to drink a toast."

Drinking goblets were made of wood, pewter, leather, or silver. Servants would bring a drink when asked, and the glass would then be rinsed in a communal basin and used for the next person.

For authenticity, you might explain this custom to guests and leave the glasses on a sideboard so they can replenish their own drinks during the party.

TABLE DÉCOR

In Shakespeare's day the dessert table was decorated with sculpted walnuts, tiny baskets, or miniature fruits and animals all made of marzipan or marchpane, as that sweet almond paste was then called. You can give your guests small jars of marzipan and invite them to create their own Elizabethan treats. You might discover hidden artistic talents as you see how much fun adults can have playing with their food!

While flowers were not generally set out onto an Elizabethan table, there is no reason you cannot include flowers at your feast. Taking a stroll through an art museum or leafing through books on still-life painting of the era can inspire your floral arrangements.

REFRESHMENTS

. . . . .

Kitchens were far away from the dining halls and food was, by necessity, served at room temperature. Many gourmets today prefer food at room temperature and suggest that it improves flavor. Serving all foods at room temperature certainly reduces a host's anxiety, as the food can be prepared before guests arrive.

Most of the recipes in *Shakespeare's Kitchen* can be prepared just prior to your party and are delicious eaten at room temperature.

"The English Husbandmen eate Barley and Rye browne bread, and preferred it to white bread abiding longer in the stomack . . . but Citizens and Gentlemen eate most pure white bred." Written in 1617 by John Murrell, this quote aptly differentiates the classes by dining customs. Farmers and laborers needed the more filling, slow-burning calories of hearty dark breads, while the upper classes ate lighter white bread. White bread was made much as we make it today, with flour, water, salt, and yeast.

In the Middle Ages the top slice of a loaf of bread was served to the most esteemed guest at the table. It is from this practice that we get the expression "upper crust," meaning the elite. By Shakespeare's time it was considered elegant to serve only individual small rolls to diners.

SHE WAS FALSE AS WATER.

Othello, 5.2

Water in Shakespeare's England was not reliably safe to drink and even the word *water* was often symbolic of falseness and lies.

According to health author Andrewe Boorde, writing in 1542, water is "unwholesome taken by itself, for Englishmen."

So, for strict authenticity, do not allow your guests to drink a drop of water! Ply them instead with fruit cider, hard cider, ale, beer, sherry, and, of course, red and white wines, which were considered essential to digestion.

CURTAIN CALL

. . . . .

ENTERTAINMENTS

THOSE PALATES . . .

MUST HAVE INVENTIONS TO DELIGHT THE TASTE . . .

Pericles, 1.4

Hosts have welcomed guests into their homes for centuries. Every good host, but especially the Elizabethan host, tried to delight and entertain guests with special foods and surprises of all sorts. Thomas Hill, in his 1567 book, *Naturall and Artificiall Conclusions,* explained "how to make an egg fly about, a merry con-

clusion," by putting a flying bat into an emptied goose egg, and "how to walk on the water, a proper secret," by attaching empty drums to your feet and seeming to glide over the water.

Most colleges and high schools have a Shakespeare society and regularly perform his works. You might invite an actor or two from a local theater company or college to perform, or ask guests to act out favorite scenes.

During great feasts pages might read passages from ancient Greek and Roman writers. Guests too were expected to recite poetry or sing. Songbooks such as *A Banquet of Dantie Conceits* (1588), containing assorted ballads, were available. One song asked what has the strongest influence over men: wine, women, or the king.

> O WHAT A THING OF STRENGTH IS WINE:
> OF HOW GREAT POWER AND MIGHT:
> FOR IT DECEIVETH EVERY ONE,
> THAT TAKES THEREIN DELIGHT.

Paul Hentzner, a German travel writer visiting England in the late 1500s, wrote of the English, "They excel in Dancing and Music, for they are active and lively."

There are many recordings of Elizabethan music that can serve as background music during your dinner. If you prefer livelier music, select the tunes from one of the Shakespeare-inspired musicals such as *Kiss Me Kate* or *West Side Story*.

ATTIRE

You might suggest that guests wear actor's basic black to your Elizabethan party and provide them with props for dress-up. Thrift shops, tag sales, and borrowing from local theater groups, schools, or dressmakers can yield some innovative finds.

STAGE DIRECTIONS

. . . . .

TABLE TALK

. . . LET IT SERVE FOR TABLE-TALK;
THEN, HOWSOE'ER THOU SPEAK'ST, 'MONG OTHER THINGS
I SHALL DIGEST IT.

The Merchant of Venice, 3.5

Elizabethan etiquette and "table-talk" books gave advice on how to engage in light banter, make puns, tell proverbs, riddles, and even jokes during dinner.

And of course, besides riddles, jokes, and puns, sparkling conversation was cultivated in ladies and gentlemen and scintillating verbal exchanges were expected among guests.

By far the most valued aspect of a feast was the chance for conversation and laughter. The Elizabethan guest enjoyed the chance to chat with neighbors, hear news of far-off places, and exchange witty banter. Laughter was so valued that medical texts discussed its benefit to health and digestion. Books such as *The Philosopher's Banquet* by Michael Scott (1614) were published listing jokes and riddles for guests to tell at dinners and feasts. Bawdy riddles such as this one were shared at feasts.

THUS MY RIDDLE DOETH BEGINE:
A MAYDE WOULD HAVE A THINGE PUT IN,
AND WITH HIR HAND SHE BROUGHT IT TO:
IT WAS SO MEEKE, IT WOULD NOT DOE:
AND AT THE LENGTH SHE USED IT SOE,
THAT TO THE HOLE SHE MAKE IT GOE.
WHEN IT HAD DONE AS SHE COULD WISHE,
"AH, HA!" QUOTH SHE, "I'ME GLAD OF THIS!"

The answer to the riddle was that the maiden was threading a needle.

Short humorous sayings were told, such as this one about lawyers.

HERE LIES A MIRACLE: DENY IT WHOE CAN:
HE LIVED A LAWYER, AND AN HONEST MAN!

Bawdy poems were recited, like this one about a new bride's conversation with her physician on sex.

A WANTON WENCH, BEINGE NEWELY WEDD
UNTO THE PLEASURES OF A MARRIED BEDD,
ASKT THE PHISITION, 'WHICH HE THOUGHT MOST RIGHT
FOR VENUS SPORTES, THE MORNINGE OR THE NIGHTE.'
HE ANSWERED HIR AS HEE DID DEEME MOST MEETE:
'THE MORNE MORE WHOLESOME;
BUT THE NIGHT MORE SWEETE.'
'NAY THEN,' QUOTH SHEE,
'SITH WE HAVE TIME AND LEASURE,
WEE'LE TOO'T EACH MORNE FOR HEALTH,
EACH NIGHT FOR PLEASURE."

THE CURTAIN GOES UP

.....

FOR NOW WE SIT TO CHAT AS WELL AS EAT.

The Taming of the Shrew, 5.2

The following bills of fare are suggested with the hope they will inspire you to gather friends and share a meal, laughter, and conversation—things just as important today as they were four hundred years ago.

POMP AND CIRCUMSTANCE:

.....

RENAISSANCE DINNER PARTY

FIRST COURSE

Dried Plums with Wine and Ginger–Zest Crostini (page 18)

"Pears" in Broth (page 38)

Renaissance Garden (page 66)

SECOND COURSE

Red Snapper with Caviar (page 180)

Sweet Pea Purée with Capers (page 109)

Renaissance Rice Balls (page 30)

SWEETS

Sweet Beets in Puff Pastry with Crème Fraîche and Ginger (page 211)

Baked Apples with Cinnamon "Stems" (page 219)

MIDSUMMER NIGHT'S DREAM:

. . . . .

PICNIC SUPPER

Spring Lettuce with Chive Flowers (page 68)
Chicken Plum Pie (page 126)
Beef Purses (page 5)
Sautéed Mushrooms "in the Italian Fashion" (page 89)
Spring Pea Tortellini (page 13)

SWEETS
1610 Rose Cakes (page 201)
Citrus Tarts (page 221)

ALL THE WORLD'S A STAGE:

. . . . .

BUFFET WITH IMPROV ACTING AND READINGS

Individual Meat Pies with Cointreau Marmalade (page 7)
Pâté with Dates and Homemade Nutmeg Mustard (page 28)
Herb Tart (page 23)
Salmon in Pastry (page 171)
Scallops in Berry Glaze (page 191)
Watercress with Roasted Parsnips (page 74)
Puréed Carrots with Currants and Spices (page 87)

SWEETS
Apple Tarts with Candied Orange Crust (page 216)
"Queen Elizabeth's Fine Cake" (page 204)

SWEETS TO THE SWEET:

. . . . .

FRUIT, CHEESE, AND DESSERT PARTY

Platter of cheese and fresh fruit
Renaissance Cookies (page 228)
Banbury Cake (page 210)
King James Biscuits (page 206) with Assorted Marmalades and Preserves

Dessert Wines
Hard Fruit Ciders

. . . FEAST HERE AWHILE,

UNTIL OUR STARS THAT FROWN LEND US A SMILE.

Pericles, I.4

I used the language of the theater in this chapter because, after all, a dinner party is a kind of theater, filled with drama and excitement. As host, you are both the producer and director. Your guests are the actors and the dinner itself, the play. As scripted, planned, and staged as you try to make it, opening night will surely delight, and frustrate, with the inevitable little surprises. Burned meats, ruined desserts, or even late guests are just part of the show, part of the fun.

I hope that through this book, you will feel connected to Shakespeare and his world in an entirely new way and perhaps be moved to take the stage with a Shakespearean feast of your own.

Bibliography

A Booke of Cookerie. Otherwise called: The good Huswifes Handmaide for the Kichin. London: Edward Allde, 1597. In the Folger Shakespeare Library Collection, Washington, D.C.

Boorde, Dr. Andrewe. *A Compendyous Regiment or a Dyetary of healthe.* W. Powell, 1567.

Buttes, Dr. Henry. *Dyets Dry Dinner.* Printed by Thos. Creede for Wm. Wood, 1599.

A Closet for Ladies and Gentlewomen. Printed in London for Arthur John, 1614.

Cogan (also Coghan), Thomas. *The Haven of Health: Chiefly Gathered for the Comfort of Students, and Consequently of All those that have a Care of their Health.* London: 1584, 1636.

Cooper, Joseph. *The Art of Cookery Refin'd and Augmented.* London: 1654.

Coryate, Thomas. *Coryates crudities; hastily gobbled up in five moneths travels.* 1611.

Culpeper, Nicholas. *Culpeper's complete Herbal.* First published by Peter Cole, 1652, under title of *The English physitian.*

Dawson, Thomas. *A book of cookerie.* London: Printed by F. A., 1629.

———. *The Good Huswifes Jewell.* London: (1585?), 1586, 1587, 1596, 1610.

———. *The Second Part of the Good Huswifes Jewell.* (1585), 1587, 1597.

Elyot, Sir. Thomas. *The Castle of Health.* Printed for the Company of Stationers, 1610.

Evelyn, John. *Acetaria: A Discourse of Sallets.* London: 1699.

Fettiplace, Elinor. *Elinor Fettiplace's receipt book: Elizabethan country house cooking.* Edited by Hilary Spurling. London: Viking Salamander, 1986.

Gerard, John. *The Herball or General Historie of plantes.* Gathered by John Gerard of London, master in Chirurgerie. London: 1597.

Good Hous-wives Treasurie, The. Printed by Edward Allde, 1588.

Good Huswifes Jewell, The. London: Printed by E. A. for Edward White, 1610.

Good Huswives Handmaide for Cookerie in her Kitchin. Printed for E. Allde, 1588.

Good Huswives Handmaide for the Kitchin, The. London: Printed by Richard Jones, 1594.

Harrison, William. *The Description of England.* London, 1577.

Holinshead's Chronicle 1. Reprint edited by F. J. Furnivall. London: New Shakespeare Society, 1877.

Longe, Sarah. *Mistress Sarah Longe her Receipt Book.* Circa 1610. In the Folger Shakespeare Library Collection, Washington, D.C.

Markham, Gervase. *Country Contentments.* London: Printed by I. B. for R. Jackson, 1623 and 1626.

———. *The English Huswife.* London: Printed by John Wolfe for Edward White, 1587.

May, Robert. *The Accomplisht Cook.* Printed in London for O. Blagrave, 1685.

Murrell, John. *A New Booke of Cookerie.* London: 1617.

———. *Murrells Two Bookes of Cookerie and Carving.* London: Printed by M. F. for John Marriot, 1631. And London: 1638.

Oxford English Dictionary (OED). London: Oxford University Press, 1971.

Partridge, John. *Delights for ladies, To adorne their Persons, Tables, Closets, and Distillatories; with Beauties, Banquets, Perfume, & waters. Reade, Practice, & Censure.* London: (1600?), 1602, 1608, 1623.

Plat, Hugh. *The History of Art and Nature.* 1594.

Plat, Sir Hugh. *A Closet for Ladies and Gentlewomen.* London: 1608.

———. *Cookerie and Huswiferie.* 1603.

———. *Delightes for Ladies.* London: 1602, 1603, 1609.

Scappi, Bartolomeo. *Opera di M. Bartolomeo Scappi, cuoco secreto di papa Pio Quinto divisi in sei libri.* Venice: 1570.

Scott, Michael. *The Philosophers Banqvet . . . The second Edition newly corrected and enlarged, to almost as much more.* By W. B. Esquire. London: Printed by T. C. for Leonard Becket, 1614.

The Treasurie of Hidden Secrets, Comonlie called the Good Huswives Closet of Provisions. 1633.

Vaughan, William. *Naturall and Artificial Directions for Health.* London: 1600.

W., A. *A Booke of Cookrye.* London: Edward Allde, 1587.

Wilson, C. Anne. *Food and Drink in Britain from the Stone Age to Recent Times.* London: Constable, 1973.

Rosemary Croutons, Seafood Soup with, 44
Saffron Toast, Veal with Glazed Grapes on, 32–33
stale, food served on, 56
toasted, added to beer and wine, 142, 251
Brillat-Savarin, Jean Anthelme, xv
broth, 51
  Almond-Orange, 45
  "Pears" in, 38, *39*
butter, 21, 219
Buttes, Henry, 163

C
cabbage(s), 100
  with Smoked Duck, 100–101
  Winter Salad with Raisin and Caper Vinaigrette, *72*, 73
cakes:
  Banbury, 210
  "Queen Elizabeth's Fine," 204–5
  Rose, 1610, 201–3, *202*
Candied Citrus Peel, 237–38
candles, 250
caper(s):
  Crab with Garlic and, 176–77
  Mint Sauce, Roast Leg of Lamb with, 143–45
  and Orange Salad, Mediterranean, 76
  Oysters on Spinach with, 25–27, *26*
  and Raisin Vinaigrette, Winter Salad with, *72*, 73
  Sweet Pea Purée with, 109
capon(s), 117
  with Peppercorn and Onion Stuffing, 115–17, *116*
carbonado, origin of term, 159
carp, 193
carrot(s), 65, 87
  Grilled Tuna with Sweet Onions and, *80*, 81–82
  Puréed, with Currants and Spices, 87
  and Shrimp Salad, 63–65, *64*
carving, 117, 138
Castle of Heatlh, The, 117
cauliflower:
  Baby, in Orange-Lemon Sauce, 102, *103*
  Chowder, 46, *47*

Caviar, Red Snapper with, 180–82, *181*
Cervantes, Miguel de, 55
chargers, 56
Cheesecake "in the Italian Fashion," 230, *231*
chestnuts:
  Beef Stew with Onions and, 57–58
  Fish Bisque with Artichokes and, *40*, 41–42
chicken(s):
  Almond Saffron, in Bread, 131–33, *132*
  and Artichokes, 120, *121*
  changing into capons, 117
  Plum Pie, 126–28, *127*
  with Sorrel Pesto, 134, *135*
  Stock, Renaissance, 240
  Velvet Soup with Grapes, 37
  with Wine, Apples, and Dried Fruit, 118–19
chile peppers, 98
Chive Flowers, Spring Lettuce with, 68–70, *69*
chocolate, 232
Chowder, Cauliflower, 46, *47*
Church of England, 24
citrus:
  Cream, Prawns in, 20–21
  Peel, Candied, 237–38
  Tarts, 221–23, *222*
cockatryce, 114
Cod Steaks with Onions and Currants, 193–94
coffee, 232
coffins (covered pies), 93
Cogan, Thomas, 36
Cointreau Marmalade, Individual Meat Pies with, 7, *8*
Comedy of Errors, The, 52, 165
conversation, 255
cookbooks:
  Elizabethan, viii–ix, 88
  of late 1700s, vii
cookies:
  Renaissance, 228–29
  1610 Rose Cakes, 201–3, *202*
Coriolanus, 159
Cornish Game Hens with Sage, 123–25, *124*
Coryat, Thomas, 174–75
"Courage" Tart, 214–15

crab(s), 176
  with Capers and Garlic, 176–77
  with Pistachios and Pine Nuts, 16, *17*
Crostini, Ginger-Zest, Dried Plums with Wine and, 18–19
Croutons, Rosemary, Seafood Soup with, 44
Crusades, 99
cucumber, in Winter Salad with Raisin and Caper Vinaigrette, *72*, 73
Cuisinier François, Le, 21
currants, 87
  Banbury Cake, 210
  Cod Steaks with Onions and, 193–94
  Puréed Carrots with Spices and, 87
  Roasted Pheasant with Wine and, 113–14

D
dates, 97, 139
  Lemony Sweet Potatoes with, 97
  Pâté with Homemade Nutmeg Mustard and, 28–29
deer hunting, 150
Delightes for Ladies, 236, 238, 239, 240
desserts, 199–232
  Apples, Baked, with Cinnamon "Stems," 219
  Beets, Sweet, in Puff Pastry with Crème Fraîche and Ginger, 211, *212*
  Cheesecake "in the Italian Fashion," 230, *231*
  Cookies, Renaissance, 228–29
  Gooseberry "Foole," Foolproof, 208
  Inside-Out Pie, 225–27, *226*
  King James Biscuits, 206
  origin of word, 218
  Quinces, "Orient Red," 224
  see also cakes; tarts
Don Quixote, 55
Dough, Renaissance, 239
dried fruit:
  Chicken with Wine, Apples and, 118–19
  Lamb Chops with Ale and, 139–41, *140*
duck:
  Breast with Gooseberries, 129
  Italian Pea Pottage, 48–49
  Smoked, Cabbages with, 100–101

ABOUT THE TYPE

This book is set in Fournier, a typeface named for Pierre Simon Fournier, the youngest son of a French printing family. He started out engraving woodblocks and large capitals, then moved on to fonts of type. In 1736 he began his own foundry and made several important contributions in the field of type design; he is said to have cut 147 alphabets of his own creation. Fournier is probably best remembered as the designer of St. Augustine Ordinaire, a face that served as the model for monotype's Fournier, which was released in 1925.